Mission: Middle America
☆ ☆ ☆ ☆ ☆ ☆ ☆ ☆ ☆ ☆ ☆

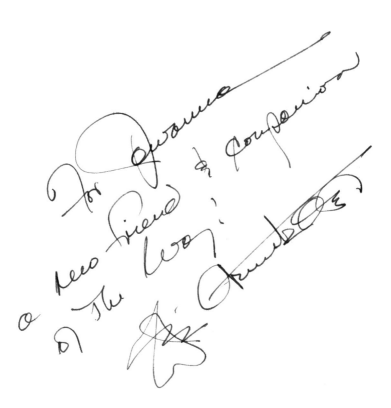

MISSION: MIDDLE AMERICA

JAMES ARMSTRONG

Abingdon Press   Nashville / New York

MISSION: MIDDLE AMERICA

SET UP, PRINTED, AND BOUND BY THE
PARTHENON PRESS, AT NASHVILLE,
TENNESSEE, UNITED STATES OF AMERICA

For

the United Methodists of
North and South Dakota
who have understood, supported
and encouraged my ministry
among them

Contents

Foreword

Is the church losing its nerve? Many signs point that way. Declining attendance, declining income, timidity, collapsing national structures, collapsing ecumenical structures; all these signs point to a loss of confidence—the church's confidence in itself, the people's confidence in the church.

We wonder where the Spirit has gone? Astrology, Zen Buddhism, Jesus Freaks show the people's religious longing, but the churches are emptying. Many of our religious leaders are fearful, blaming our social involvement, blaming our updating of sexual morality, blaming the modernizing of the liturgy. Like most fearful men they are retreating and in retreat are losing the little confidence they have. Or, in a panic, they seek superficial panaceas.

Thank God, Bishop Armstrong is not one of these. You will find in this book mainline, orthodox Christianity set squarely in the world where the cross was planted, and where Jesus walked and taught and healed and struggled and died. And you will find here an honest book that faces the weakness of the church and the corruption and suffering of the world without blanching.

The chapters range across the problems we all discuss: religious activity outside the church, the absurdity of religious sectarianism, the desperate need for reconciliation. We walk through Middle America guided by a proudly confessed Middle American and, through the eyes of a native, see its chauvinism as well as its patriotism, its self-reliance as well as its xenophobia. Armstrong clearly points to the humanity beneath skin color, the courage behind the beard. With him we cringe at the horror of Vietnam and are inspired to redouble our effort for peace.

This book is Middle America preaching to Middle America. The thrilling thing about it is that the message pulls no punches; the Bishop totally believes that this unadorned, tough and realistic gospel will be received by his audience as *good news*.

Bishop Armstrong has a record of action to back up his words. He is intellectually competent, politically aware; and he is one who perseveres in his difficult vineyard, the heart of institutional Christianity. And he is a gentle man. I have had the pleasure of working with him and have known the quiet strength of his companionship.

You will find no tricks here, but the real thing. I am glad there is one great church leader who has not lost his nerve. Instead, Jim Armstrong preaches right on. This gives all of us hope and power.

PAUL MOORE, JR.
Bishop Coadjutor, Diocese of New York
Protestant Episcopal Church

Introduction

One of the chapters included in these pages is called "Mission: Middle America." That chapter provides the theme for the book. More important than converting Chinese communists or Sudanese Muslims to the Christian faith is the challenge of converting American church members. As a Middle American I am convinced that my kind of people in my kind of church will either find true liberation and new life in Christ or will fail the present hour.

New life in Christ leads to far more than warm feelings and personal blessedness. It requires a fresh way of looking at things and profound new levels of commitment. The chapters that follow deal with the crucial issues of the day: conventional values in a different sort of world, politics and polarization, an environment grown hazy and foul, military madness, Indochina, and civil disobedience. Most Protestant Christians are Middle-American (the term has little to do with geography), and most of our churches are shaped more by cultural influences than by divine grace. Thus it is imperative that the Middle-American church member be confronted with the searching implications of the gospel of a living Christ. Either that gospel will be related to the life-and-death issues before us (and they are literally that), or we can write the church off as a meaningless relic of a bygone day.

Some will argue that these chapters are too problem-centered. They may feel the author should have dealt more with themes of grace and redemption. I understand the fundamental importance of these themes and have tried, in chapters two, three, and four, to deal with the sources of Christian experience, conscience, and action. But the time has come to relate the bedrock dimensions of our faith to the specifics of a harsh and complex world. For the sake of the human story, God's self-revelation must be *applied*.

Middle Americans have much in common with the Pharisees of Jesus' day. The Pharisees had begun as a people's movement in an hour of national crisis. As time passed, they grew complacent, defensive, and self-consciously "religious." Jesus must have had great hope for them. He gave less time to the revolutionaries (Zealots) and the intellectual elite (Sadducees). He mingled freely with the Pharisees, talked with them and pled with them to "repent and be converted." His judgments may have seemed harsh (see Matthew 23), but they were based on the obvious conviction that God needed the Pharisees and that it was not too late for them to turn away from double standards and unworthy loyalties to become faithful and obedient servants. The same can be said for Middle America.

There are qualities of true greatness in Middle America. I am profoundly thankful for my beginnings in its soil and my present relationship to it. I pray that those of us who are a part of it may be open to the will of God as he tries to lead us into ways of radical change and essential new life.

Religious Man in the Seventies 1
☆ ☆ ☆ ☆ ☆ ☆ ☆ ☆ ☆ ☆ ☆ ☆ ☆

Many years ago Quincy Howe said, "The twentieth century has put the human race on trial for its life." There is a sense in which this decade—the 1970's—will determine the outcome of this trial. Will we set in motion those processes and programs that can save our environment? Will we be able to control exploding population statistics? Will world leadership put the needs of the human family above cheap manipulation, paranoid rhetoric, and political survival? Will we acknowledge the legitimacy of the demands for radical change to be heard on every hand? Will we think, choose, and act on the basis of this knowledge? Will we be able, in the light of current madness, to stop this side of some nuclear Armageddon?

Man is on trial for his life, and his recent past only confuses matters. *Newsweek* magazine said it this way: "We . . . have set too much in motion, have disturbed our institutions and ourselves too greatly to have any very clear ideas about how things will turn out." [1] You see, the pressures of history—here-and-now, this-minute history—are forcing us to rethink the investment of our energies, the arrangement of our priorities, and the organization of our society.

We are coming to see that our basic institutions—our economic systems, political parties, agencies of government, strategies of management, the mass media, and educational and religious structures—are a major part of the problem. We are preoccupied with and are, in large measure, at the mercy of the institutions of our society.

I can enjoy the refreshing impiety and searching judgments of Robert Townsend's book *Up the Organization,* but as a churchman (a bishop, no less) it is assumed that I am first and foremost an "organization man." Right now my desk is piled sky-high with institutional claptrap. There is a stack of booklets and correspondence dealing with COCU, the Church of Christ Uniting. There is the proposed "plan of union." There is a resource booklet for studying the plan of union. There are materials related to the liturgy, theology, and polity of the plan of union. There are letters, impassioned pleas from denominational executives, telling me to "get on board." Ecumenicity is the wave of the future, they argue. I hope so—although COCU and our ecumenical future are not necessarily one. I am a delegate to the World Council and the National Council of Churches. I am involved in the reorganization of the councils of churches in the two states I serve. But really! How long will we assume that we are automatically doing the will of God when we dismantle, reassemble, and lubricate ecclesiastical (or any other kind of organizational) machinery. Colin Morris, long a central figure in British ecumenical circles, came to a fork in the road not long ago and took an unexpected turn. He wrote: "I have undergone something of a conversion on the question of Anglican-Methodist Union. . . . I don't give a damn which way the vote goes." He went on to say:

I don't really care whether I end up in a Union Church or as a residual Methodist. I don't really care whether I am ordained, re-ordained, reconciled or commissioned by Bishops, Presidents, priests or presbyters. . . .

I'm willing to go through that Service of Reconciliation kneeling, standing, sitting or laying flat on my face. . . .

Is it not time we distinguished between what is genuine and what is spurious in our present concerns? . . .

If I am not humanly useful to the life of the world then the laying on of hands of every Bishop in Christendom will not validate my ministry.[2]

If I am not humanly useful in the world—there you have it! There are matters of greater import than redesigning the organizational charts and rearranging the furniture within the cozy walls of our institutional fortresses.

Some time ago I sat in a senator's office on Capitol Hill with a young friend who was urging the senator to come into his state and enter the 1972 presidential primary. The young man, a university professor, is doing what he can to salvage and redirect his party in that state. At one point in the conversation he said, "You've got to come, Senator. If the Party, if the political process is going to be saved, we have to break free from self-interest, get off this patronage kick, and have an 'issue-oriented' campaign." Issues should be of profound importance to Christians too. *To be "humanly useful" and to be "issue-oriented" are requisites for all of us in the 70's.*

We can dabble endlessly with nonessentials if we choose. Meanwhile, back in a very real world, the rights of citizens are violated, freedoms are denied or repressed, air and water are poisoned, multitudes go to bed hungry every night, race warfare rages, revolutionary terrorism spreads, and we totally disregard the ultimate law-and-order issue—world law and world order. We fiddle—and Rome continues to burn. One of our nation's most distinguished public servants has written:

No true Christian is deserving of peace of soul who does not address himself to the hard issues of war and peace, Vietnam, the arms race and international community. No Christian worthy of the name can feed his own soul without concern for those around him who hunger in body and spirit. No Christian can really commune with his Creator, who denies the dignity of his fellow creatures by reason of race or class or creed.[3]

Religious man in the 70's is called to veer away from irrelevant busyness and institutional self-centeredness that he might, in the genuineness of his own selfhood, respond to persons in need.

I have quoted Colin Morris at length. Do you know why he took the turn he took? He was president of the United Church of Zambia. One day an African native dropped dead not a hundred yards from his front door. The man had starved to death. The pathologist found a few blades of grass in the man's stomach, nothing else. Morris wrote:

Though [that] little man . . . has scorched my conscience, he has at least freed me from my faithless worrying about the survival of the Church. . . .
Now I know that the survival which counts is not that of the Church but of the little man with the shrunken belly.[4]

The church exists to give itself away; to offer itself for others. If it thinks primarily in terms of its institutional well-being, it might well lose everything—except its "respectability." There would have been no resurrection, no promise of new life, had Jesus not first been willing to die for the least of this earth.

Voices from unexpected places sometimes call us back to truths too long ignored. Nearly ten years ago the SDS was founded in Port Huron, Michigan. That was before Berkeley and Columbia, before the Weathermen and Chicago's Days of Rage. The Port Huron Statement, the founding manifesto of the SDS, contains some lines that should be read and heeded by young terrorists and defensive church leaders alike:

We regard men as infinitely precious and possessed of unfulfilled capacities for reason, freedom and love. . . . We oppose the depersonalization that reduces human beings to the status of things. . . . Loneliness, estrangement, isolation describe the vast distance between man and man today. These dominant tendencies cannot be overcome by better personnel management, nor by improved gadgets, but only when a love of man overcomes the idolatrous worship of things by man.[5]

These words stress a neglected core of New Testament truth. Human progress and survival are made possible not by theological nit-picking or ecclesiastical game-playing, not by the passage of high-sounding and prophetic resolutions, but by unselfish love offered to flesh-and-blood people in the concrete circumstances of their daily lives.

How far institutional religionists have strayed from the genius of their founder! In his "inaugural address" (see Luke 4) Jesus said that he had come to preach to the poor, proclaim release to the captive, and set at liberty those who are bruised. He did not just *say* the words, he *lived* them. Talk about liberation! The Samaritans were the hated and disenfranchised of his day. He was there with them. Adultery was the most degrading of sins. He was there with her. Publicans, sinners, winebibbers, gluttons—he was not "too good" for them either. The establishments—Pilate and the high priests, Rome and Jerusalem, church and state—he defied. He talked about the most radical forms of love: forgiveness, going a second mile, turning the other cheek, overcoming evil with good, loving the enemy—and he spelled them out in his own attitudes and relationships. And finally he died, not the natural death of obscurity, but the martyr's death, the death of one man for others.

As we face the unprecedented demands of the 70's, we need to take far more seriously than most have the lowly man from Nazareth who fashioned a movement that turned the world upside down.

The apostle Paul once said, "God . . . has chosen what the

world calls weak to shame the strong" (1 Cor. 1:27 Phillips). Theodore Roszak, in his important book *The Making of a Counter Culture,* talks about the "absurdity" of the Christian triumph. It was a triumph of "absolute nobodies, the very scum of the earth, whose own counter culture was . . . little more than a scattering of suggestive ideas, a few crude symbols and a desperate longing" [6]—*a desperate longing.*

Quincy Howe said, "The twentieth century has put the human race on trial for its life." But man has a desperate longing to survive; not simply to stay alive, but to survive with justice, freedom, and peace; to survive with dignity and integrity, with his personhood intact. A letter recently received from a university student put it this way: "With the question of extinction now open what can man look to as a future? We must have a future if there is to be sanity."

It would be appropriate to talk about the church in the 1970's, but, because of an assortment of popular hang-ups, that doesn't seem to be enough. Too often when we think of the church, we think of a building on a corner, a man in a black robe, a gathering of well-dressed, middle-class Americans who sing songs and pray prayers totally unrelated to everything else they represent. That is not the church of the future. Oh, there will still be buildings and songs and prayers, but there will also be open spaces, crowded tenements, and the language of the world; guitars and drums as well as Bach, sweet-tempered sounds and the shouts of liberated souls. No single class or race will dominate, no single form prevail. No single structure can hold the truth of the Spirit.

The church of tomorrow will be a church of Sacrament and Word, yes, but it will also be the body of Christ entering the world, becoming a part of the travail of the world, giving itself to and for the world. It will bring together the foolish and wise; the weak and strong; culture and counter culture. It will reach out to embrace those persons and groups who struggle and sacrifice for peace, who fight for justice; those who offer themselves for the waylost, the brutalized, and the drug-sated. The church will not only provide sanctuary and grace for the respectable, it will be a rallying point and source of strength for the struggling, outnumbered, misunderstood "nobodies" who seek to build a different kind of world in which old things have passed away and all things have been made new.

This is why, instead of thinking only of the church in traditional ways, we are talking about *religious man* in the 70's. Religious man—not orthodox or patriotic or educated or righteous man, but religious man—for religious man is that person who looks beyond himself for meaning and tries to find his place in the total scheme of things.

Religious man knows there is transcendent reality beyond earthbound objects and creature things.

Religious man knows that human beings can be neither defined nor contained; they are persons of incalculable worth.

Religious man knows that parties, movements, causes, and institutions are all measured and judged on the basis of their effect upon persons.

Religious man believes in the liberating power of love; in freedom as love's expression and justice as love's demand.

Religious man lives not for the state alone, not for himself alone, but for the sake of brother man. And brother man is *every* man.

Religious man learns from the past but is not bound by it. He respects authority without being intimidated by it. He is kind, gentle, and unashamedly "good," but he is also strong. And in the presence of forces of evil, he is aggressive and untamed. Coretta King, paying homage to her slain husband, said: "My husband healed more broken souls and bodies with his direct fighting message than thousands of his colleagues accomplished with pallid sermons addressed to half-empty pews." [7]

I believe that religious man finds his highest fulfillment in Jesus Christ as Lord. Mrs. King went on to say:

Jesus preached in the streets, especially to the poor and the slaves. He did not timidly and ambiguously imply the brotherhood of man: He proclaimed it. He did not mildly disapprove of war: He blessed the peacemakers. He did not worry about his popularity with the rich and the powerful: He scorned them for their indifference and greed. The church, if it would keep the allegiance of the young, will have to rediscover Jesus, the radical. [8]

Religious man will not be threatened by words like these but will respond to them, knowing that the hour is late and that we are but one mistake away from extinction.

"The twentieth century has put the human race on trial for its life." These years through which we now move are of supreme importance. "My brothers, think what sort of people you are, whom God has called." (I Cor. 1:26.) We are called to be the servants of man; messengers of reconciliation. God is our righteousness. In him we are consecrated and set free. In his grace we will find the strength and resources to help this good earth fulfill its wondrous promise.

In the First Place ... 2
☆ ☆ ☆ ☆ ☆ ☆ ☆ ☆

Let us begin with a handful of axioms:

One, the church (*your* church) exists to give itself away.

Two, at the center of the Christian imperative stands the person Jesus Christ.

Three, in his life, death, resurrection, and continuing influence Christ reveals the will of God and the human potential. He shows us what we are meant to be.

Four, the Nazarene can literally transform life. He can turn the individual around, making of him a new creature. He can cleanse and redirect the structures of society.

Five, it follows, therefore, that the first and fundamental task of the church is to possess, experience, and share the life, spirit, love, and power of Christ. Everything else is secondary.

Now if we really believed all this, ours would be a different sort of world. But we don't—and it's not. Leighton Ford once said, "I bow my head in shame when I contrast the tame Christian I am with the bold Christian I should be. I am much more like Snoopy, daydreaming on top of the dog house about fighting the Red Baron, than I am a daring revolutionary." [1] In this, I fear, he speaks for most of us.

When I was a young preacher, one of the churches I served liked to sing a gospel jingle that included the words:

> Christ is the answer
> To all of our problems;
> He holds the key
> To the whole world's peace.

I confess I used to smirk at what seemed to be the naïve dogmatism of those words. No longer. We have tried more sophisticated ways, and they have failed. As a churchman I must acknowledge that my failures have come when I have not taken Jesus Christ seriously enough. As a human being I need to understand that my earthbound and eternal destinies are all wrapped up in him.

The church has always said it, but today—from a fresh, demanding perspective—we need to reaffirm it: *Jesus Christ is our Lord and Savior.* He is the source of the new life we seek. He is our point of beginning.

Maybe one of the reasons our lives seem so empty and our relationship to the church so frustrating (and sometimes maddening) is because we have not *started* with Christ. In spite of our rich traditions many of us have no firsthand knowledge of the meaning of Christian experience and commitment. We play religious word games, but we literally do not know what we are talking about. Christ remains for us a proper name in a hymnbook or a creedal statement. He is a Sunday school hero, a Christmas decoration, a sacred name on saintly lips, but not a living part of our present experience. E. Stanley Jones, after spending sixty years visiting churches the world over, says that only about one out of three church members he has observed seemed "converted."

Our churches are facing unprecedented crises, we are told. Roman Catholics are confused by Vatican II, angered by the pope's statements on birth control, and bewildered by liturgical reform and the Berrigans. In 1970 the Catholic Church in the United States showed a membership decline for the first time in seventy-five years. Protestant churches are facing a pocketbook pinch. The Protestant Episcopal Church has had to cut back its national staff by half. Lutherans are drastically reducing their field staff. The Billy Graham Evangelistic Association suffered an 8 percent loss of income. Most mainstream denominations have been affected by this withdrawal of persons and support.

A host of reasons are given for the statistical setbacks. Business recessions intimidate churches as well as other institutions. There are people who are unhappy with the ecumenical movement, who are blaming Vatican II, the World Council of Churches, and the National Council of Churches for the woes of organized religion (usually these unhappy folk are sinfully misinformed). And there has been "confrontation politics": Cesar Chavez in California, James Forman in New York, Phil Lawson in Kansas City, and all the others. While critics argue that the churches have become too involved, too worldly, others argue that they are not worldly enough. They insist that churches have been unwilling to identify sufficiently with the tragic pain and urgent conflicts of the hour. Many reasons are given for the churches' apparent failures. I am convinced that there is one fundamental cause giving rise to all others. *Our churches are troubled and divided today because they are not "in Christ," and they are not "in Christ" because so many of us are not "in Christ."* Our inner worlds churn with anger and bitterness; our voices are caustic and critical; our attitudes deny warmth and trust and love. We have not claimed for ourselves the peace and joy of a vital faith. The policies and strategies we call for deny the radiant confidence of obedient discipleship.

We can ridicule the jargon if we choose, but the fact remains, we are not what we ought to be, doing what we ought to do, laughing, loving, sharing, risking what we ought to risk, giving what we ought to give because we have not been "born again"—born into worlds of new attitudes, motives, values, and relationships. "When anyone is united to Christ, there is a new world!" (II Cor. 5:17.)

In the first place, before grappling with institutional crises or grave social problems, we are called into vital fellowship with a living Christ. But then what? Then reconciliation. First, Christ—then reconciliation. The church in mission experiences the indivisibility of the two: Christ and reconciliation. There is no living Christ apart from reconciliation. "God was in Christ reconciling, . . . he has entrusted us with the message of reconciliation. . . . We implore you, be reconciled to God!" (II Cor. 5:18-20.)

Reconciliation. Is such a message needed in today's world? You know the answer.

The Middle East is embroiled in bitter conflict, splintered by irreconcilable differences.

Paris negotiations are anything but negotiations, as antagonists stare at one another across a table, rejecting overtures, hoping to wear down the "enemy," and waiting for a trip to China to undo twenty years of history and produce a miracle.

Cambodia is another Vietnam. Two years ago a Cambodian official said, "If the Americans come they will cause untold destruction and misery. They will kill a few [Communists], . . . but they will kill Cambodians too and when they are gone the [Communists] . . . will return." [2] He was right. The Americans came—and went. But the Communists are still there and Cambodians are still dying. Now Laos, yet another helpless, primitive country, has been battered into rubble. Republican Congressman Paul McCloskey returned from Laos a few months ago to talk about the destruction of 3,500 villages in the northern region.

Since 1960, thirty new African nations have come into being. Coincidentally, during that period of time there have been thirty coups or armed uprisings in those nations. There have been major civil wars in the Congo and Nigeria. There are vicious racist governments in Rhodesia and South Africa. Tribal conflicts and liberation skirmishes continue to erupt.

The Middle East, Southeast Asia, Africa, *and Latin America.* Chile, with its newly elected Marxist government, is on the

Left. Brazil, with its military dictatorship, occupies the Right. And a continent, poised between the two ideologies, stands confused and ambivalent in the face of external pressures and internal unrest.

Look at our own troubled land. True, urban ghettoes have simmered down and campuses are quieter, but we remain a seriously divided nation: rich against poor, young against old, conservative against liberal, country against city, white against people of color. Have you read Dee Brown's *Bury My Heart at Wounded Knee,* "an Indian history of the American west"? Don't read it unless you are prepared for the mutilation of Cheyenne and Arapaho women and children; unless you can take in stride the Sand Creek massacre. Geoffrey Wolff, writing about the book, says:

The books I review, week upon week, report the destruction of the land or the air; they detail the perversion of justice; they reveal national stupidities. None of them—not one—has saddened me and shamed me as this book has. . . . Reading it has made me realize for once and all that we really don't know who we are, or where we came from, or what we have done, or why.[3]

The history of man is the story of irrational destruction, of violent racism, of pillage, rape, exploitation, and war. The story continues to unfold as our planet smolders and threatens to destroy itself.

"God was in Christ reconciling the world unto himself." Do we need the message? You know the answer. Yet the only alienation is not that "out there"—in Vietnam or Harlem or on the Rosebud Reservation in South Dakota. It is within us. Many of us need to know the meaning of reconciliation. We feel betrayed and alone. There are the grief-stricken or the neglected elderly. There are the young who want to be heard and understood; who want to be treated like persons. There are the "isolates": students, divorcées, bachelors, widows—yes, and husbands and wives—who live in their isolated compartments, walled off from one another, trying to tolerate one another in homes that have become emotional jungles. Some of us would give almost anything if we could feel a touch of gentle love; hear a tender voice; be enfolded by another person's accepting and unselfish warmth.

We need to remind ourselves that the ultimate source of love is not within us. It springs neither from our generous spirits, nor from our neurotic needs. The source of love is *God*. Reconciliation, then, begins with him. Thus, the wisdom of Paul's admonition "be reconciled to God." To receive the love of God as revealed in Christ is to refashion the whole realm of life and relationship. *In the first place—Christ.*

Even after considering the brokenness of the world, we return to Christ, and to ourselves. We are weaklings who need strength. We are sinners who need forgiveness. We are arrogant and need humility. We are broken and need to be healed. We are separated from one another and from our truest, deepest selves. We need to be reconciled. Paul Tillich, in his best-known sermon, talked about reconciliation, reunion, and resurrection. The "new being," Tillich said, is reconciled to God and reunited with himself. Suddenly he realizes that he is "eternally important, eternally loved, eternally accepted. Now there is a center, a direction, a meaning of [his] life." [4] This is what it means to be saved.

Salvation cannot be grasped and smothered by the individual alone. It must be offered and applied to the larger, fragmented world of which he is a part. Christ said he had come not to condemn the world but to save it. If the world is to be saved, the gospel of reconciliation must be radically applied to culture; to technological developments, economic systems, and political movements; to the institutions that shape man's earthbound destiny. The church, then, must view itself as a reconciling body seeking to bring the hostile forces of this world together.

As an extension of Christ's reconciling work in this moment of time, the church will stand opposed to those voices that needlessly divide us, whether they belong to the vulgar racist, the violent revolutionary, or those who cling to a cherished status quo. The church will oppose irrational anarchy, whether on city streets, on troubled campuses, or in the foreign policy of the United States. The church will stand opposed to injustice wherever it appears; to tyranny, oppression, cruelty, immorality; to the brutalization of persons; to anything that dehumanizes.

An obedient and faithful church will not necessarily be a popular church with overflowing treasuries. But then Jesus did not function on the basis of consensus. He died on a cross.

Remember—

The church (*your* church) exists to give itself away.

At the center of the process stands Jesus Christ.

In his life, death, resurrection, and continuing impact, Jesus reveals the will of God and our own possibilities.

Jesus can literally transform life. He can take any one of us and turn us about; make of us new persons. And he can cleanse and redirect the currents of history.

It follows, then, that the first and basic task of the church is to experience, possess, and share the life, spirit, love, and power of Christ. Everything else is secondary. But—and this is equally important to remember—everything else will be effected. "Everything" is what Christ died for. And "everything" is what we are called upon to serve.

3 Straws in the Wind

☆ ☆ ☆ ☆ ☆ ☆ ☆ ☆

This nation is no stranger to deep religious conviction. Puritans, Separatists, Quakers, and German pietists were among those who first sought refuge on these shores. The "great awakening" of Jonathan Edwards and George White-field swept across New England and down the Atlantic coast in the mid-eighteenth century. The so-called second awakening, spearheaded by circuit riders, camp meetings, New Light Presbyterians, Campbellites, and a new breed of preachers inspired by Charles G. Finney, came along a hundred years later. Now there are those who say we are on the threshold of a third great spiritual awakening. Maybe. There are signs of a quickened spirit abroad.

Billy Graham, with his huge crowds, his press coverage, and his Gallup Poll popularity, is a unique religious phenomenon.

Oral Roberts and Rex Humbard leap from channel to channel as they bring their brand of urgent evangelism to millions of television viewers every Sunday morning. Men with names like Brother Al, Reverend Ike and C. W. Burpo, indelicately called "the God-hucksters of radio," [1] appeal to hundreds of thousands of "soul-hungry" Americans day and night.

Campus Crusade and the Fellowship of Christian Athletes recruit wholesome young mid-Americans and, last year, the Asbury "revival"—beginning in a regular chapel service in Hughes Memorial Auditorium—touched student groups from California to South Carolina, from Oklahoma to Saskatchewan.

If well-scrubbed, clean-shaven young Americans are responding to the lure of the spirit, so are long-haired, bearded ones. The "Jesus movement," with its "soul clinics," street preaching, and counter culture Fundamentalism, is bringing a word of grace to the disenchanted and unwashed multitudes.

These "signs" I have mentioned have been headline grabbers, and, for the most part, they have conformed to traditional patterns of revivalism. Beyond them, and more important than any isolated manifestations, are certain trends, "straws in the wind," that suggest God's powerful action in our midst.

There appears to be genuine healing taking place between warring members of the Body of Christ. Forces, long antagonistic, are developing a new though sometimes grudging respect for one another. You know the sad history of the past seventy-five years, with sharp lines drawn between a social gospel and a personal gospel; between pietist and activist. No one is more nauseating than a smug, self-righteous, arrogant, convinced religionist, and there has been a lot of nausea in sacred circles over these past years.

Today we hear about the marriage taking place between evangelicals and "worldly" Christians. Such talk is nonsense. A marriage requires two separate bodies and the gospel is one. Paul said, "Christ is like a single body . . . [and] we were all brought into one body . . . in . . . one spirit" (I Cor. 12:12-13).

We are not, therefore, talking about the marriage of separate entities, we are talking about a healing process taking place within this one body of ours. Nausea, induced by intellectual and spiritual arrogance, is not the basic sickness. The basic sickness is schizophrenia. The church has developed a split personality.

On the one hand, the old-style Fundamentalist said:

"You must accept my view of the Bible, of justification

and sanctification, of the Second Coming, or you won't be saved."

"You must come to Jesus my way, or you won't be saved."

"You must believe a particular set of doctrinal proposi- tions, or you won't be saved."

"Modernists," they cried," are the antichrist."

Modernists, on the other hand, said:

"Science is the new messiah."

"We must outgrow the primitive and archaic; we must have done with superstition and magic."

"On the basis of *our* insights and ingenuity we are called to build a new man in a new world."

"The Fundamentalists? The Fundamentalists are illiterate obstructionists," they charged.

So the battle raged between "warring" members of the same body. It was, and is, a disgraceful battle, sinful, wasteful, and, in the light of desperate human need, inexcusable.

Jesus told us to love God *and* man. That, he said, is *one* law.

He said, "You must be born of the spirit" *and* "you must feed the hungry, clothe the naked, and deliver the op- pressed." That is *one* gospel.

Jesus died for our sins, true. He also died because he posed a threat to the political leadership of his land. These are not contradictory statements. They are parts of the same larger truth.

Those who would limit our Lord's ministry to wonder- working and soul-seeking have missed the point as truly as those who would confine his role to that of a raging revolu- tionary. He was both, and more—infinitely more.

This truth is coming to us; we are understanding and ex- pressing it as we have not before. Dudley Ward, General Secretary of United Methodism's Board of Christian Social

Concerns, has been labeled a dangerous radical by a few uninformed elements within the church. Recently, in a radio interview, he said, "The gospel is a whole. A false dichotomy exists. There is not both a social and a personal gospel. They belong together." Professor Claude Thompson, speaking at the first Good News Convocation in Dallas, said: "I am disturbed because of two groups in the Church. The radical activists put all the emphasis on social action but have little Gospel. . . . On the other hand, . . . evangelicals—especially conservative fundamentalists of the Bible belt—. . . have little social vision and less social action." He added, "I want both the activists *and* the pietists to see the failure of their half-gospels." [2] They are beginning to see. *We* are beginning to see. The body is being healed. The *oneness* of Lord and faith are being affirmed with confidence and power.

Another straw in the wind: *There is a new sensitivity to the presence of the eternal spirit; the Holy Spirit.* Many are coming to understand in new ways what Wesley meant when he said, "The best of all is, God is with us." Ours is a here-and-now God, a *living* God.

The growth of Pentecostal churches is one indication of this new interest in and emphasis upon the Holy Spirit. Yet their growth in the United States, remarkable as it sometimes seems, is nothing compared to the mass Pentecostal movement in Latin America. In Chile and Brazil the major Pentecostal groups have a much larger constituency than all the historic Protestant churches combined. Social scientists can explain this Latin-American phenomenon by talking about the predominance of the lower classes, the high rates of illiteracy, the mysticism of "folk Catholicism," and the Latin-American temperament. But these are not the only factors. Emilio Willems, an authority on Latin-American Christianity, has described the contagious force of Pentecostal worship:

The repentant believer may expect the descent of the Holy Spirit *here and now.* . . . He comes to the individual person. . . . Communion with or seizure by the Spirit is an everyday experience which may be observed whenever the members of the congregation gather for religious services. There is nearly *always* someone who has visions, speaks in tongues or prophetizes.[3]

One Sunday night I worshiped in a large Pentecostal church in São Paulo, Brazil. The church had no paid clergymen. That night more than three thousand people were there. Some prayed in tongues, some testified, and finally one of the elders of the congregation was led by the Spirit to preach. God's presence was *assumed* in that gathering. That morning I had attended another Pentecostal church, Manoel de Melo's "Brasil para Cristo," where nearly ten thousand were present. Healing services were in progress. The congregation was young and enthusiastic. A pulsating mood of exuberant joy filled the air. To these people, many of them simple and unlettered, God was no theoretical abstraction, no theological proposition; he was *their* refuge, *their* savior; *their* deliverer; *their* strong protector. Religion was not something to be studied or debated. Rather, God was available to be possessed and to possess.

This awareness of the Spirit, however, is not limited to Pentecostal sects. There have been outbursts of glossolalia at Duquesne and Notre Dame universities in the United States. Some time ago, *The National Catholic Reporter* said, "At . . . private gatherings a growing number of Catholics have been experiencing the same 'baptism in the Spirit' that Protestant pentecostals experience." [4] For the past decade the Protestant Episcopal Church has been experimenting with healing services and has been experiencing new dimensions of the Spirit. Recently I preached in a United Methodist church in Sioux Falls, South Dakota. Following the service a fine-looking man introduced himself as a visitor from Nebraska. With a smile on his face he said, "I'm a spirit-filled Methodist. Praise God!" Just like that—to a bishop, in a sedate church of my denomination. He was sharing out of the overflow, and we were talking as brothers in Christ. As Marcus Bach has recently written, "The Holy Spirit is no longer a sectarian possession but a universal expression." [5]

I mentioned the exuberant joy of the Pentecostal church in São Paulo that Sunday morning. Do you know how the service began? For the first two or three minutes wave after wave of applause swept across the congregation. "The people are greeting Jesus," I was told. Nothing dull and stereotyped about that worship. Thousands of people were rejoicing in the presence of *their* living Lord.

That is another straw in the wind. Not only are activists and pietists drawing together, not only is the Spirit of God at work in our midst, but *a contemporary Christ is being recognized and taken seriously by the multitudes.*

Judy Collins and Joan Baez have not been identified with the conventional church, yet their sensitive and searching renditions of "Amazing Grace" and "Just a Closer Walk with Thee" were being played by disc jockeys everywhere not long ago. And the hungry and impatient young were listening. *Jesus Christ Superstar,* a rock opera by two men in their twenties, became an overnight sensation a few months ago. Performed by artists from the casts of *Hair* and *Cabaret,* as well as a lead singer from the Deep Purple group, this eighty-seven-minute composition offers views of Judas, Pontius Pilate, Mary Magdalene, and Jesus that are both compelling and provocative. It will soon be made into a movie. A secular world is *seeking,* and the illusive and mysterious Nazarene is looming larger and larger in the quest.

And there are the Jesus Freaks; the Children of God with their soul clinics and their new life. Most of these youngsters had been hooked on sex and drugs, but they have broken free.

Oh, they haven't returned to a "straight" society. They reject the materialism and hypocrisy of their parents' worlds and their parents' churches. They don't want to go through empty motions and play games with God. But they have been "liberated," their former life-styles no longer enslave them, and they are devoting their energies to the building of a new kind of community where work and possessions are shared. Bible study, meaningful witness, and personal growth *in Christ* are stressed. These young people are radical puritans, far more like New Testament Christians than most of us.

Bethel Tabernacle is in North Redondo Beach in southern California. Over the past two years fifteen thousand young people, most of them on drugs, have passed through its doors. At least four thousand of these kids, with the help of Christ, have kicked the habit. Describing their new life a reporter says, "Drugs are the common leveler. . . . [But] Christ is the great common denominator. He brings everyone together." [6]

Christ—"superstar" to the rock generation, healer and deliverer of the hooked generation—is also a brother to the revolutionary. I saw the posters on a wall not long ago. There was Che, martyr/hero of the Latin-American revolution. There was Huey Newton, Black Panther leader. There was Jesus of Nazareth, whose followers "turned the world upside down." Why not? The Christ who defied Annas and Caiaphas, who refused to bow his knee to Rome, and who drove money changers from the Temple is surely no partner to the poverty and hunger, the vicious racism, economic imperialism, and insane warmaking of our time. Nonviolent? Yes. Loving? Yes. Revolutionary? *Yes!*

Talking about the spiritual reality of Latin America, John Mackay has said, "The church needs today a fresh vision of Jesus Christ, a new experience of the light and power of the

Gospel, together with total dedication to the task of making Christ and the Gospel known to contemporary man throughout the world and relevant to all his problems." [7] If there is to be an authentic spiritual awakening, Jesus Christ must be the transforming reality in its very center. Otherwise it can swing off in a thousand irresponsible directions. History warns us—

Religious awakening can offer little more than escape from unpleasant reality and harsh, demanding responsibility.

It can manipulate feelings and exploit emotions.

With extravagant talk of promise and reward it can be as grasping and self-centered as pagan sin.

It can be used by the political charlatan for his own purposes.

It can be bound up with the demonic goals of fascism, racism, militarism, and nationalism.

In other words, a religious awakening, harnessing unbelievable energies, can go where its charismatic leaders take it. If it is of God it must be defined, controlled, and empowered by the living Christ. Thus it will be *his* and not ours.

I thank God for the straws in the wind! Evangelicals and social activists are praying and marching together. The Holy Spirit is working in his marvelous, unpredictable ways, cleansing, empowering, healing, unifying. And Jesus Christ refuses to be isolated to the realms of myth and ancient history. He is here—now—swinging, moving, searching, cleansing, leading us into whatever the future holds.

4 A "Full" Gospel
☆ ☆ ☆ ☆ ☆ ☆ ☆

What does the phrase "full gospel" mean? To the Pentecostalist, it means the Holy Spirit and faith healing; the Holy Spirit and speaking in tongues; the Holy Spirit and perfect love. It means the baptism of the Holy Spirit; the indwelling of the Holy Spirit; the continuing witness of the Holy Spirit. Beyond justification, it means sanctification.

Many who talk about a full gospel assume that people who disagree with them have an empty gospel or, at best, only half-a-gospel. Sometimes full gospel advocates are frightfully narrow and self-centered. They thank God for his saving and keeping power, but are quite certain he saves and keeps only their kind. They argue that unless you have experienced what they have and feel what they do, you are only a partial Christian. Grateful for the promise of heaven, they seem blissfully unaware of the hell that often exists in the world around them.

I believe in a full gospel—not in the full gospel of the Pentecostalist, though we have much to learn from his openness to the Spirit and the intensity of his quest. I believe in the full gospel of Jesus Christ; the full gospel of the new covenant. The gospel of Christ traces its roots back into the soil of Hebrew law and prophecy. It was anticipated by John the Baptist in the wilderness, in the waters of the Jordan, and in the presence of a weak and hateful king. It moved from a tradesman's bench into the swirling crosscurrents of a hostile world, identifying with the down-and-out while defying the up-and-in. It loved, accepted, forgave, suffered, and died on a cross, but it refused to stay dead. The *kerygma*—the good news of God in Christ—is the bold truth the church embraces and proclaims. To do less or to do otherwise is to betray the fullness of the gospel.

The *Manifesto for the Renewal of the Church* rightly insists that "the renewed Church must be as faithful to the biblical reality that brings it into being as to the world that calls it into service." The biblical reality that brings the Church into being calls for a wholehearted response to God's self-revelation in Christ.

I remember the kind of preaching I heard in my boyhood. It was emotional: laughing, weeping, whispering, shouting. It pled and threatened and cajoled. It had many blind spots and tended to skirt controversy. But with all its weakness and its extravagant enthusiasm, it drew much of its authority and power from the Bible. Again and again, that preaching referred back to Moses and a burning bush, Amos and a lion's roar, Isaiah in the temple, Jeremiah in an almond orchard, and Paul on the Damascus Road. It was forever repeating the urgent question of the Philippian jailer, "What must I do to be saved?" The God it described was an active God, working in and through persons and events, demanding the obedient response of the individual.

Because my background was Wesleyan, it placed much stress upon religious experience. How often I heard stories of Augustine and his praying mother; Augustine and a bird in a garden; Augustine and his old friend and mentor Ambrose. And there was Martin Luther and a thunderstorm; the sale of indulgences; the devil's inkwell; justification by faith. And there was John Wesley and Aldersgate. When Wesley's name was mentioned, everything else seemed to recede into the background, and usually allusion would be made to a London prayer meeting in May of 1738 when the little priest's "heart was strangely warmed" and he came to *know* that his sins were truly forgiven. Much emphasis was placed upon sin, penitence, and salvation; upon law and grace; and upon the disciplines of the holy life. (More often than not, in the preaching I heard, these disciplines prohibited smoking, dancing, movies, gambling, drinking, and even card playing, but were seldom, if ever, related to race prejudice, economic injustice, chauvinism, and war.) Great stress was placed upon the witness of the Spirit, perfect love, and personal holiness. Little was said about social justice.

Looking back, I can appreciate the biblical emphasis upon conversion and new life; the inescapable demands of a personal gospel. But I regret that the *fullness* of Wesley's contribution was left unexplored. No mention was made of his impact upon prison reform, the slave trade, rum-running, and the labor movement. Many who consider themselves "Wesleyan" do not realize how far-reaching and inclusive his thought and ministry were. (Wesley had his flaws. Not until my student days did I learn that Wesley, as a churchman, was a rigid sacramentalist and an absolute autocrat; as a political animal he was a staunch Tory who took an exceedingly dim view of the American Revolution; and as a husband he was a flop—which means we had better not limit our understanding of a "full gospel" to any mere mortal, however revered and historically significant he may be!)

The faithful application of the biblical reality that brought the church into being requires a profoundly personal response. Certainly Claude H. Thompson asked an essential question when he wrote: "I favor the total involvement of the Church in social action, social revolution. But suppose we do all this and fail to help people *become Christian?*" [1] Exactly so. But what does it mean, in a world like ours, to "become Christian"? The easy shortcuts of partial gospels must be exposed and scorned. The full gospel calls us to present *ourselves* as living sacrifices, to heed the words of one who said, "If any man will come after me, let him deny himself, take up his cross daily, and follow me." To *follow* Christ into grimy marketplaces and temples turned commercial, into sinners' hangouts and Samaritan ghettoes, into Gethsemane and Pilate's presence and up to Calvary is not the same as getting a perfect attendance award or buying a life membership in the Women's Society of Christian Service. A young Mennonite scholar has said it like this:

To be Christian is to be an extremist. . . . Christian faith is not a halfway measure; it talks about going two miles instead of one, of plucking out eyes that disturb, of dying on a cross. It is to risk death, to love enemies and to pray without ceasing. . . . [The Christian] does the good regardless of consequences or effectiveness. Faith involves intensity and commitment. We are called to love God with our whole being." [2]

As the *Manifesto for the Renewal of the Church* reminds us, biblical reality calls us into being; *the world* calls us into service. Servanthood is a central aspect of the biblical reality and of a full gospel. Dag Hammarskjöld, in an oft-quoted phrase, said the obvious: "In this era, the road to holiness necessarily passes through the world of action."

In talking about "Straws in the Wind" I mentioned Manoel de Melo and the Brasil para Cristo movement. Those who assume all Pentecostalists are otherworldly escapists have little knowledge of "Brasil para Cristo." It has soup kitchens, sewing classes, clothing distribution centers, employment services, and a plethora of welfare programs. It sponsors political candidates (Levi Tavares, one of the most respected Federal Deputies and a member of the opposition party, is a lay preacher in Manoel's São Paulo congregation) and is a member of the World Council of Churches. Manoel de Melo is one Pentecostal leader who understands that the road to holiness and the world of action are one.

Dom Helder Câmara, another Brazilian, represents, as few men in our time, the fullness of the gospel. Heroic Archbishop of Olinda and Recife, he was nominated for the Nobel Peace Prize in 1970. For years he has led the Brazilian Catholic Church in its witness to young progressives, the working masses, and lowly peasants. He has mingled with, and sought to influence, makers of public policy and has courageously identified with victims of public policy. Since 1965, he has cried out against repression in his beloved land and has brought the torture of political prisoners to the attention of a shocked world. His government has sought to defame and discredit him and refuses to let the Brazilian press quote him or make reference to him. Speaking at the opening of a seminary in Northeast Brazil a few years ago, he said:

You cannot evangelize abstract creatures, intemporal, existing in a void. When our seminarians get to the churches and chapels and speak of divine grace . . . how can they forget that they are proclaiming divine life to listeners who very often live in subhuman conditions? . . . To persist in a purely spiritual evangelization would soon result in giving the impression that religion is something separate from life and powerless to touch it or overcome its absurd and erroneous aspects. It would even tend to support the view that religion is a great alienating influence, the opium of the people.[3]

I met and talked with Dom Helder in his episcopal "palace" (a rambling, rundown structure in the heart of Recife) last winter. We discussed the generals' revolution and political repression. At one point in our conversation he said, "Far worse than torture is the lack of human development in Brazil. Our people need to be lifted up; *humanized.* They live in houses that are not houses. They have no clothes, no money, no freedom. They live in a subhuman world." A full gospel refuses to "save" those people while remaining blind to the conditions that damn them to suffering and servitude.

Dom Helder understands that "humanization" and "salvation" are different ways of referring to the same process. If society dehumanizes the individual it literally destroys him. Persons need to be converted (turned around); so do the institutions and structures that define the limits of their selfhood.

It is a half-gospel that seeks the conversion of the soldier while ignoring the war economy and war system that set the stage for Vietnams, arms races, and nuclear destruction.

It is a half-gospel that seeks the conversion of the black or red man while tolerating subtle and blatant forms of racism that confine millions of his kind to worlds of hopelessness, fear, and violence.

It is a half-gospel that seeks the conversion of the unemployed or unemployable while condoning and blessing economic systems that encourage the rich to get richer at the expense of the poor even as two-thirds of this earth's people are hungry.

There is no legitimate way for the Christian to extract the individual from his surroundings. To try to convert individuals while assuming no responsibility for the laws that shape their lives and the systems that govern and limit their destinies is to repeat an all-too-familiar and comfortable heresy and to betray the gospel of our Lord. The faithful will refuse to be drawn into a personal *versus* social gospel debate. There is no either/or choice to be made. Rather, we will try to proclaim and demonstrate a *full* gospel, a *whole* gospel, a gospel that calls persons to repentance and conversion and that judges the civil rights laws, welfare programs, and foreign policies of nations. The full gospel knows both depth and outreach. It is experienced *and* applied. It is dependent upon reflection and prayer and is on intimate terms with misunderstanding, hardship, and conflict. It relates to every aspect of life.

Bruce and Eugenia Johnson, a young preacher and his wife, were sent to work in a rundown neighborhood on Chicago's near North Side. They sought out and tried to help defeated people crowded in nearby tenements. They opened their church basement (and their hearts) to hurt and angry street gangs. They met each week with other Christian workers in Chicago and talked and prayed about the crucial issues of their city: racial tension, drugs, urban renewal, politics, and community organization. They were sometimes misunderstood. They received threatening letters and phone calls. But they continued their ministries of involvement and reconciliation until one October night in 1969, when they were brutally murdered in their tiny apartment.

Two days later the shocked community paid tribute to their memories. The funeral procession was a half-mile long. More than two hundred clergymen marched alongside Young Lords and Black Panthers. Hippies and straights were there together. Smartly dressed suburban matrons walked quietly with haggard mothers from Appalachia who carried little children with tattered clothes and runny noses. As the people reached the old church, balloons were released, symbolizing the power of love over hate; of life over death.

One of the speakers at the memorial service was a young Puerto Rican. Obviously this was a new role for him. His voice trembled, but his words were eloquent. He said:

Bruce came down from the mountaintops of the rich to be with the poor. He was not a regular minister but . . . 'slick-talking, cool,' the way we do in the ghetto. Sometimes we read about Jesus Christ and forget what he came for, . . . to free men's souls, to free men spiritually and physically. . . . Most people are like boats in a harbor, always tied up to the dock. Bruce and Eugenia left the harbor and tried to cross the water.[4]

And the people said, "Amen."

Jesus, calling the first disciples, challenged them to "launch out into the deep" (Luke 5:4). He offered them no safety in the harbor. They were wrenched from familiar and secure ways and sent as servants into hostile worlds. Sometimes frightened, sometimes wavering, they followed their Lord. Dusty roadways, teaming marketplaces, Samaritan villages, and cross-crowned hills became their homes. They came to know rejection, imprisonment, and even martyrs' deaths, but their faithful obedience changed forever the story of man. Responding to the claims of a full gospel, they gave themselves as living sacrifices. *We are called to do the same.*

5 Mission: Middle America
☆☆☆☆☆☆☆☆☆☆☆

Who is Middle America? A fist-swinging hard-hat on Wall Street? John Wayne? Bob Hope? That now-legendary forty-seven-year-old housewife in Dayton, Ohio?

Where is Middle America? In Chicago with "hizzoner" Mayor Daley and the *Tribune,* or on the Potomac in the Pentagon, or at San Clemente with its "White House" tucked away from the disquieting realities of that other house on Pennsylvania Avenue?

What is Middle America? The "southern strategy" of Kevin Phillips? The Social Issue of Richard Scammon? The security blanket of the fed-up and the frightened?

Middle America: Richard Nixon's waspish answer to the underdog coalitions of FDR and JFK; "Squaresville's" reply to the counter culture.

Since ours is, for the most part, a Middle-American church, we need to analyze Middle America prayerfully and critically. Let me be defensive at the outset. Middle America cannot be all bad. Too many of us are a part of it. Every boyhood memory I possess is a Middle-American (Hoosier, to be exact) memory: Fortville, Syracuse, Spiceland, Lake Wawasee; the depression; a red brick schoolhouse and a musty church basement; picnics and dime stores and farmyard smells.

The only religion I knew as a boy was a simple, sometimes-shouting, often-confused Protestantism. Catholics were foreigners who lived in cities. Jews had long noses and belonged in the Old Testament.

The only race I knew was white. Oh, the town where my grandfather lived had a black barber. I spent long hours with Ellis, a Negro cook at a Boy Scout camp. I had a distant cousin, an old woman doctor, who took me with her when she made her calls in "niggertown." She always made me wait in the car.

I was taught to love the USA. On George Washington's two hundredth birthday (I was in the second grade at the time) I was the Father of our Country in a school play. The Fourth of July was a very special holiday. I don't remember much about the rhetoric and pageantry, but there were firecrackers, ladyfingers, torpedoes, rockets, cap guns, sparklers, and Roman candles. On Memorial Day we put flags on the fenders of the car and drove a hundred miles to visit the family cemetery. Invariably we children would be told about "Uncle Andy," an infantry captain shot between the eyes a few weeks before Armistice Day in 1918.

I peddled the *Saturday Evening Post*, the *Ladies' Home Journal* and the *Country Gentleman*. My boyhood was described a hundred times by Sinclair Lewis. It was given color and form by Grant Wood and Norman Rockwell. As I look back, the pieces seem to fit together, and the memories are pleasant and wholesome.

There was much that was good in that world: a warm and basic family life, a three-R's kind of school that had a playground used for play and teachers who loved to teach, and a church that sang lusty songs, quoted the Bible, prayed self-righteously, and was beginning to experiment with maps, scissors, and paste. Our patriotism was naïve and unquestioning. It was assumed that hard work and clean living would bring success. Tom Swift and Horatio Alger had not yet receded into the archives of an oversimplified, overdrawn past.

What has happened to the Middle America of my boyhood

days? I will tell you exactly what has happened. It has lost its innocence. Voices of helpless poverty have shamed self-centered prosperity. Voices of black self-consciousness have shattered racist presuppositions. Urbanization and industrialization have changed forever the leisurely and protected warmth of Main Street. Uncontrolled technology and massive corporate structures have swallowed up the persons in our midst. People have become pawns in the hands of systems, movements, and machines. And patriotism? Patriotism has lost its innocence, too. McCarthyism, the Pentagon, the CIA, and, more than anything else, Vietnam have seen to that.

The Middle American, once so comfortable and secure, is now a shaken and often belligerent man. Not long ago *Newsweek* magazine offered a special report on "the man in the middle [the troubled American who] is giving vent to his frustration, his disillusionment, and his anger." [1]

This man who looks and talks like so many of us has never had it so good. He works hard. He plays hard. He has a split-level house and a two-car garage. But he is miserable. His innards are boiling over. Policemen are being shot, bombs are being exploded, kids are smoking pot and making love, black people refuse to stay in their "place," and the strongest nation in the world is not permitted to win a little, grassfire war. In a sense, Eric Hoffer, the longshoreman, is Middle America's philosopher in residence. He barks: "You better watch out. . . . The common man is standing up and someday he's going to elect a policeman President of the United States." [2]

He is not doing badly, Hoffer's common man. He has the power of the nation in his pocket. The White House is *his.* The Pentagon is *his.* The police and courts are *his.* The economy is *his.* He has been in the driver's seat a long time, and he is not about to surrender his place. He is not about to voluntarily share his wealth with the poor. He is not about to voluntarily share his schools, churches, unions, or social status with blacks. He does not want to share his country with people who question, ridicule, or deny his values. He does not want to share his world with communists or other "dangerous," hungry challengers of the status quo. He has a special thing about hippies, black militants, welfare mothers, and campus revolutionaries, and he has suddenly realized, as one of his number cries, that he "outnumbers, outvotes and could, if he chose to, outgun the fringe rebel."

What has all of this to do with life in our churches? I am convinced that much of today's tension in the religious community stems from the common assumption that the American church is but one facet of the so-called American way of life. When church leaders or denominational policies seem to challenge the patriotic assumptions of Middle America, "all hell breaks loose." After all, has not the American church always been an *American* church, from Elder Brewster and the Rev. John Witherspoon right up to Cardinal Spellman and Billy Graham?

Today, in part because of our confusion and divisions, a national consensus religion seems to be gaining strength.

More and more people are worshiping at the shrine of God *and* country. While paying lip service to the sovereignty of God and the universal lordship of Christ, they do, in fact, bow down before a strange assortment of national, regional, military, and political idols.

The cross and flag stand side by side on their altars, but the flag always seems to stand a bit taller and its claims and disciplines seem more binding (especially on the young) than the claims and disciplines of the cross.

This national religion has its own social gospel. It specializes in phrases like "law and order" and "anti-communism." The Middle-American religionist may think Carl McIntire and Billy James Hargis are pretty far out, but stability *is* more important than justice, isn't it? And collective security *is* more important than individual freedom, isn't it? Should we let the communists win in Southeast Asia?

To many the kingdom of God and the American way of life are virtually synonymous. Our economic system is sacrosanct. Our foreign policy, always the product of benign goodwill, is above reproach. Anyone who questions presidential decisions or military priorities is not only disloyal but unchristian as well.

The symbolic locus of this national religion was a football stadium (naturally) in Knoxville, Tennessee, during the political campaign of 1970. A Billy Graham revival was underway. The President of the United States happened, by chance, to be passing through. Our national leader and national chaplain stood side by side before the multitudes. Nonpolitical? Of course it was nonpolitical. The fact that Senator Albert Gore, distinguished public servant but foe of the war in Southeast Asia, was uninvited though in town, while William Brock, of Chattanooga chocolate fame, Gore's opponent in a crucial senatorial race, was seated in the shared spotlight on the platform should not be permitted to confuse the issue at all.

People who used to turn purple at the mere mention of the initials FDR or JFK now piously insist that the first of the Ten Commandments is "Thou shalt support thy president." They vaguely remember the words, "Thou shalt have no other gods before me," but that kind of religious imperative cannot hold a candle to Stephen Decatur's toast: "My country, right or wrong." A religious news editor, writing me not long ago, suggested that, in his view, the greatest threat to America's well-being is not a repressive police state on the right, or a violent revolution on the left, but the most dangerous of all heresies—"nation worship."

Following the General Conference of my denomination in 1968, a conference that supported civil disobedience under certain conditions, a Cincinnati woman shook an angry finger in her pastor's face and cried, "I just want you to know, I love my country more than I love my church." Her name is legion. However, she needs to understand, as we all do, that both her church *and* her country are under the continuing judgments of God. (Have we forgotten so soon the lessons of Hitler's Germany and Stalin's Russia?) I know of a preacher who once knelt during a worship service and kissed his nation's flag. Did he understand the heresy involved? When a woman wrote a letter to the editor of the *New York Post* in the summer of 1968 attacking the World Council of Churches for not preaching "the blood of Christ" and the "American way of life," did she understand the implications of her complaint?

In these days of national crisis it is extremely important that we differentiate between civil religion and the Christian faith. The civil religion of Rousseau was a common-denominator religion, expressing belief in a beneficent God, eternal life, the happiness of good men, the punishment of the wicked, and the sanctity of the laws of the nation. I am afraid that a host of Middle-American church members, hearing those sentiments expressed, would say, "Well, that sounds 'Christian' to me." Yet, there is no mention of Jesus Christ, of faith or grace, of the cost of discipleship, of love or justice or the demands of the cross and the promise of new life. Middle America appears to have much more in common with Rousseau and Rotary than with the man from Nazareth.

Lest you misunderstand, let me say it again. Most of *us* are Middle-American to the core. The history we have studied is a biased, chauvinistic history. (This is true of people in every nation.) The religion we have known has been influenced far more by cultural and racial considerations than we care to admit. (This has always been true.) We have been spawned and shaped by frightfully narrow worlds. But we are in this thing together, and no one of us possesses that spiritual or ethical preeminence that permits him to "talk down" to another.

If the church is Middle America in microcosm, then it follows that the church is the number one mission field of the church. The task of evangelism begins with *us*. Before we can get into all the world teaching and healing, we need to face up to, and be liberated from, our own racism, materialism, and nation worship. Nearly twenty-five years ago Karl Barth said, "The church can never escape the obligation of reconverting itself." That is where we are. What then is the task before us? It begins where Christ began, at the bedrock of genuine commitment. "Repent and believe," he demanded. *Repent and believe—*

With this starting place we are called to be "heartily sorry for these *our* misdoings." We, as churches and as churchmen, are called to the mourner's bench of agonizing penitence. We have sinned and fallen short of God's glory.

We need to acknowledge our *racism*. Oh, we don't lynch people or overturn school buses, but we do tolerate moods and co-operate with systems that demean and exploit. For the sake of harmony we permit bigotry to go unchallenged.

We need to acknowledge our *materialism*. Sinclair Lewis was right. "The dollar sign *has* chased the crucifix clear off the sky." We need to understand how many times we make decisions that protect an affluent style of life and a career-potential while denying those for whom the lowly Nazarene died.

We need to acknowledge the *hypocrisy* of our double standards. We mutter about smoking and drinking, pornography and drugs, about the rebellion of the young and the violence of the broken and defeated while neglecting "weightier matters" of justice and mercy and peace. We thrive on a politics of fear, forgetting that unselfish love—and that alone—can cope with the sources of fear.

We need to acknowledge our *callous insensitivity.* We speak loftily of the brotherhood of man, but, even as we voice noble sentiments, we turn away from the battered hulk in the ditch: the long-haired hippie, the old and senile, the angry black man, the unpleasant and unclean, the frightened and insecure, the whore, the pimp, the pusher—those to whom Jesus gave himself so freely.

We need to acknowledge the *false gods* we bow down before: flags, political messiahs, power (economic, military, and personal), unworthy causes, and the endless claims of self-interest.

Above all else, we need to acknowledge our participation in "original sin," that fundamental betrayal that gives birth to the multiforms of evil: *the sin of self-worship.* I do not care if you are learned professor, bishop, truck driver, housewife, banker, research analyst, or parish priest, there is no redemption this side of penitence. Repentance is not mere intellectual acknowledgment, it is the soul crying out for deliverance; it is the prayer of the man in the shadows, "O God, be merciful to me a sinner."

"Repent and believe." *Believe!*

Believe that God is the Father and Judge of us all and that he has made of one blood all nations.

Believe that he revealed himself in Jesus Christ who is the Savior of man and the Lord of *all* life.

Believe that Christ lived and died for the least of men, to save *us* from our sins. (And don't take this lightly. Think it through!)

Believe that Christ "rose from the dead." His eternal spirit of liberating truth is with us yet to convict, forgive, cleanse, heal, empower, and guide.

Believe that the church is the body of Christ—not merely

a social organism, much less a gathering place for nice, like-minded friends—but *the body of Christ,* here to *do* his truth at all costs among all kinds of people.

If the Middle-American church is a cultic church, it is our prime mission field. It stands in need of redemption. Since we are a part of the church, we are a part of the challenge. For that reason, the call is to us: "Repent, believe, . . . for *the kingdom of God is at hand."*

Hair, Soap, and Sin 6
☆ ☆ ☆ ☆ ☆ ☆ ☆ ☆ ☆

One summer while on vacation I grew a beard. I had always been curious and my wife and daughter goaded me on, so we let nature take its course. Depending upon her mood, my wife said I looked "interesting," or like Ernest Hemingway, or "sexy," or like Brutus, the villain in the Popeye comic strip. When vacation time was over, I returned to civilization and, much to the consternation of my loved ones, shaved the shaggy thing off.

But you know, that beard prompted some fascinating reactions. Some people stared; some muttered. One day in a grocery store a fellow snarled "hippie" as I walked past him. I discovered that there are many uptight people who are making surface judgments these days.

In Tampa, Florida, a young man was arrested for "desecrating the flag." He had not desecrated the flag. He was selling peace flags, flags with red and white stripes and peace symbols in the fields of blue. Newspapers invariably referred to him as a "bearded youth." For years Tampa Bay has boasted an assortment of fine, respectable-looking yachtsmen who have "desecrated" the flag in exactly the same way; that is, on their yachts they have hoisted flags with red and white stripes and with anchors on the fields of blue. No one has ever hauled them into court. You see, if you are a bearded youngster with political views that are unpopular in certain circles, it makes a difference.

We need to remember that long hair and beards have a distinguished if somewhat stuffy history. Can you think of three more conservative institutions than Czarist Russia, the British Empire in its heyday, and the Supreme Court of Charles Evans Hughes? Yet Czar Nicholas wore a beard, as did Britain's Edward VII and George V, and Chief Justice Hughes was the epitome of dignity with his white whiskers. Incidentally, Republican Presidents Harrison, Garfield, Hayes, Grant, and Lincoln all wore beards, and they (with the possible exception of Lincoln) were hardly considered fire-breathing radicals in their day.

According to tradition, Moses was bearded; Jeremiah was bearded; patriarchs and prophets were bearded; the apostle Paul was bearded; Jesus was bearded. If Michelangelo is to be believed, even God at creation boasted a flowing beard.

Sometime ago I saw two wirephotos on the same page of a newspaper. One picture was of Charles Manson, the self-deluded cultist, who was then on trial for his life in connection with the grisly murder of seven people. The other picture was of a young white man teaching a group of black boys how to swim in the municipal pool of a southern city. Both Manson and the swimming instructor had long hair and beards. The fact that you wear long hair and a beard does not necessarily mean that you are a drug-prone cultist, nor does it necessarily mean that you are a dedicated idealist trying to help underprivileged children. Jesus understood all that. He said, "Things that defile a man. . . proceed from the heart." It is not how often you wash, or how often you go to the barber—how you *look*—but it is your inner world. What are your motives? What are your attitudes? What are you really like inside?

One of the distinguishing features of the new covenant was the internalizing of morality. Jesus argued that appearances can be deceiving. Pharisees *appeared* to be very righteous.

They weren't. Our Lord *appeared* to be a "winebibber and a glutton." He wasn't. It is the interior life of a person that is all-important. "The kingdom of God is within." Most of us have not learned that. We judge things on the basis of what they appear to be.

Two or three years ago one of the major commercial interests in the country placed a full-page ad in the *Wall Street Journal.* It showed a fine-looking man in a business suit. Above the man's picture was the question: What is the first thing you see? A friend of mine, an insurance executive, carried that ad around with him for days asking his friends: "What is the first thing you see?" Without exception the answer came back, "a Negro" or "a black businessman." That's how I answered. We are all trapped by the tendency to see only the surface of things. We see the race of a man before we see the man in the man. We see the slant of his eyes or the red or the brown or the black of his skin, and the first, and sometimes decisive, impression is made.

The same shallow standards are applied elsewhere. We see a barefooted, long-haired youngster in blue jeans and with dirty fingernails, and we "know" who he is. We know what he is like. Or we see an elderly man with a shriveled leg and a paralyzed arm riding in a wheelchair, and again, we don't see the *person* there, the person longing for understanding and relationship. We just see an old cripple and we turn away. It is not fair! There is more to any one of us than meets the eye. We have our private worlds, our inner worlds, where the issues of life are really resolved.

In the Beatitudes, Jesus turned the attention of his followers inward. He praised those who are "poor in spirit," that is, humble, teachable, gentle. He praised those who "hunger and thirst after righteousness," who want, more than anything else, to live *good* lives. He praised the merciful, the considerate, the "pure in heart," and those who try to reconcile differences, the "peacemakers." He also said a good word for those who suffer, whether they are mourning the loss of loved ones or paying a price, in lonely isolation, for their own prophetic courage.

Later, Jesus would underscore the importance of the inner life when he compared external appearances and behavior to one's real selfhood.

Murder is evil, he said, but the deed emerges from the thought—anger, bitterness, hatred, vindictiveness.

Adultery is wrong, he said, but the deed emerges from the thought—the lust; the sensual desire that is pampered, cultivated, and entertained by the weak or the unprincipled.

A man does what he thinks. If his thoughts are careless or irresponsible or evil, his actions will reflect the climate of his inner world. Jesus said it like this: "Wicked thoughts, murder, adultery, fornication, theft, perjury, slander—*these all proceed from the heart;* and these are the things that defile a man" (Matt. 15:19).

Politicians and public figures are talking a lot these days about quality of life. There is no true quality unless one's inner world is what it ought to be. Paul, who captured so much of the genius of our Lord, said, "If you are guided by the Spirit you will not fulfill the desires of your lower nature" (Gal. 5:16). It is life guided by, dominated by the Spirit of love that produces quality living.

But the good life cannot be lived in isolation. Integrity is never expressed in a vacuum. *Jesus sent his followers into a real world to express their faithful obedience.*

My mother, now approaching eighty, lives in a planned community in southern California. It is called Leisure World. Although more than ten thousand people live there, Leisure World is surrounded by a high block wall. You must have a pass to get in. Guards at a gatehouse scrupulously check your pass. Once inside you find a near idyllic village with churches, game rooms, craft shops, baths, swimming pools, health clinics, an abundance of flags, and carefully manicured lawns and flower gardens. The average age within those walls is seventy-four. In a sense, Leisure World is ideal for those who live in it. My mother is secure and happy, and I am profoundly grateful. There is also a sense in which something just doesn't ring true. There is no risk involved; no violence or injustice or hunger. And in a real world there are risk and hardship.

A few months ago I visited Leisure World and heard many references to "long-haired hippies." I would guess that those who referred so disparagingly to their younger brothers had never known or talked with one. A few weeks earlier I had shared in a consultation with some "citizens of Woodstock." A young man from San Diego's counter culture was present. The first time I saw him I was repelled. He had a heavy, matted beard and shoulder-length hair. He was fat and slovenly. He wore a dirty sleeveless shirt, a pair of blue jeans, no shoes. I did not like some of his habits. I did not like some of his language. But as we talked, day after day, it became apparent that he had something to teach us.

He had earned a Ph.D. in Physics and had worked in a "defense" plant. There came a time when he could no longer justify his work. He was making instruments of death. His conscience rebelled, and so he quit—opted out—and went to San Diego. Now he lives on subsistence wages, working, he says, for peace and happiness. He spends half his money to rent a rambling, rundown house in the inner city where drifters and runaways are accepted and find warmth and lodging. He is simply spending his resources and energies to help people.

Now I confess the young man has certain traits and mannerisms that still turn me off, but I wonder which of our lifestyles is most like the man from Nazareth? I fear I know. No wonder Harvey Cox, and others like him, write that the flower children of today have much in common with Francis of Assisi.

Don't misunderstand. I am not pleading for slovenliness, for carelessness in language or habit. I am appalled and frightened by the deification of drugs in certain pockets of the counter culture. Inhumane violence is the antithesis of everything I read in the New Testament. This is not a plea for some particular brand of New Left radicalism. I am only suggesting that, as Christians, we owe it to ourselves and to our brother —whoever he may be—to look beyond the dress or lack of same, beyond the beard or lack of same, beyond the soap or lack of same, beyond the outward appearance, that we might find the flesh and blood *person* there.

If we could just transcend these first impressions; the way things *appear* to be. Paul talked about the clothes we wear. He said, "Put on the garments that suit God's chosen people." Then he listed them: "compassion, kindness, humility, gentleness, patience." Then he added, "Be forbearing, . . . and forgiving." And finally, "To crown all, there must be love, to bind all together and complete the whole." (Col. 3:12-14.)

Jesus internalized morality. Goodness is not what we look like, what we *seem* to be, but what we are—what we really are, inside.

A Boiling Pot, a Seething Cauldron 7
☆ ☆ ☆ ☆ ☆ ☆ ☆ ☆ ☆ ☆ ☆ ☆ ☆ ☆ ☆

Viewing his world, Jeremiah cried, "I see a boiling pot, a seething cauldron." He might have been describing our revolutionary moment of time. Hungry and underprivileged masses are in revolt. Underdeveloped nations are striking the shackles from their bodies. People, long oppressed, are demanding justice, equality, and their rightful share of this world's goods.

Revolutionary sentiments not only are sweeping across dark and long-neglected continents, but have invaded sanctuaries of civilized privilege in the Western World. Farmers riot in Belgium, students strike in Paris, and public officials are slain in Canada. In the United States, where ROTC buildings are burned and government research laboratories are bombed, Angela Davis is on trial for her life. John Dillinger types have been crowded off the FBI's Most Wanted lists by political "criminals," the Dohrns and Berrigans of a new day. Good Americans are confused. They do not know whether to believe the doctrinaire patriotism of J. Edgar Hoover or the impatient idealism of Ramsey Clark. Obviously, revolution runs deeper than the violent antics of the Weathermen.

In 1976 the United States of America will be two hundred years old. Sedate and embattled Middle Americans tend to forget that the midwives who helped bring their republic to birth were a band of youthful, long-haired radicals with honored names like Patrick Henry, Alexander Hamilton, and

Thomas Jefferson. We may be counterrevolutionaries now, but once we took pride in the individualistic life-style of the frontier, the violence of Concord and Lexington, and the bold truculence of the Declaration of Independence.

The revolutions we face today are as convulsive as Jeremiah's vision; as sweeping and manifold as those of our colonial forefathers.

There is the revolution of life-style. Culture is being challenged by counter culture.

On the one hand, there are the Puritan values and Victorian roots of an inhibited past. Sex should be kept underground, repressed, denied. Hard work, good habits, stable and well-ordered family life, and a stern-though-temperate religion set the stage for happiness; that is, money in the right banks, membership in the right clubs, a measure of richly deserved comfort, and insurance policies designed to cover any eventuality. Hair should be short, bodies clean, language decent, dress "respectable," and morals "pure."

On the other hand, there is the challenge of the counter culture. The counter culture talks about freedom; spontaneity; "putting-it-all-together." It sneers at the narrowness and hypocrisy of Victorian standards. Its hair is long, its fashions random, its language crude, and its style careless and defiant. Rebelling against the rigidity of the past, it develops its own cults of opinionated conformity.

Our churches (remember, they tend to reflect Middle-American loyalties) usually reject the overtures of the counter culture. The submarine church, the underground press, the throb of the folk festival, the "presumption" of *Jesus Christ Superstar,* and the radical idealism of the young seem to threaten and offend those who pride themselves on the strength and propriety of their orthodox convictions.

Some time ago a group of United Methodist bishops joined with a cross-section of vital young Americans to spend three days together "rapping." The youngsters were a representative lot. There were straights and freaks, dropouts and honor students, Black Panther apologists, hippies, and cleancut all-American types. Both conversation and confrontation were featured. A few of the young people seemed utterly insensitive to the feelings, experience, and piety of some of their older brothers. A few of the bishops seemed openly hostile to the questions, candor, and iconoclasm of some of the youngsters. For these very reasons, the days were valuable. We were able to experience, demonstrate, and (to a degree) resolve some of the styles and tensions that divide us. Reich's realms of Consciousness I, II, and III [1] were all present and well represented. But how is understanding to be developed and unity achieved unless we venture past the barricades of those who challenge our ways?

It would seem that culture champions duty and propriety; counter culture, freedom and celebration. If the church is not merely a class institution, if it seeks to be faithful to its founder and truly inclusive, it will experiment with, gladly embrace, and try to reflect the best of both worlds.

Revolution isn't just a matter of life-style. It has a methodology. Perhaps *the most crucial debate of the day is being waged between those who are committed to nonviolence and those who argue they are driven to violence.*

Responsible Christian's voices, many of them representing the Third World, plead for understanding in the presence of regrettable but sometimes necessary violence directed against economic, military, and political repression. Colin Morris, who has a knack for making conscientious Christians squirm, writes:

The freedom fighter, whether he operates in the Zambesi Valley or a Chicago ghetto is not introducing violence into a peaceful society. He is responding pathetically to a greater violence which is not less murderous because it is clothed in the majesty of the law. Western society is not at peace—it is in an uneasy state of equilibrium achieved by the deployment of massive force against mass indignation.[2]

Morris goes on to say an essential word:

To starve people is violence; to rob them of their dignity and self-respect is violence; to deny them political rights or discriminate against them is violence. Elaborate structures of violence make a terrorist what he is.[3]

Here at home the Black Panther Party takes up guns in what it calls self-defense. It talks about Oakland and Fred Hampton and the Soledad brothers. There is a persuasive measure of bleeding, pleading logic in its rhetoric. But before we unquestioningly accept the logic, we need to read Giap and Che and Regis Debray on the meaning of "armed self-defense" in guerrilla warfare. How far out does the perimeter of self-defense extend? When does self-defense stop being self-defense? And what about the stockpiling of dynamite, lead pipes, and homemade bombs in innocent-looking store-fronts?

The decisive revolutions of modern times—Britain, 1640; America, 1776; France, 1789; Russia, 1917; and China, 1948— have been violent revolutions. Rap Brown was incontestably right when he said, "Violence is as American as cherry pie." In 1776 we came to birth in violence. The heroes in our history books are George Washington, Robert E. Lee, Ulysses S. Grant, Stonewall Jackson, Phil Sheridan, Admiral Dewey, "Blackjack" Pershing, and George Patton, men of violence. We have been involved in every major war of the twentieth century. Today our armed frontier is worldwide; our saber rattles on every continent. I, for one, find no comfort in my President's words to Pope Paul when he left him, "Tonight after I leave the Vatican, I will be flying to sea, and there I shall see the mightiest military force which exists in the world on any ocean." Violence? We take pride in it. It is a part of us. Think back—

Whatever happened to the American Indian (Sand Creek was My Lai on a larger scale)? How did African slaves get to this continent? What was a posse? A lynch mob? The Ku Klux Klan? What was the Haymarket massacre? Who were the Pinkerton detectives? How was the National Guard used in the labor disputes of the 1930's and in Chicago in 1968 and at Kent State? What about Detroit and Harlem and Watts? Don't forget a President named Kennedy, a senator named Kennedy and a preacher named King. There were Bull Conner and his dogs, civil rights workers in Philadelphia, Mississippi, Medgar Evers, James Reeb, and four little black girls, bombed to death in their Birmingham Sunday school class. There are those—and they are many—who insist that unless cruel and blind inhumanity is met with violence, injustice will be permitted to prevail.

While we are at it, why do those who condemn street violence most vigorously close their eyes to the massive violence in Southeast Asia? Why do those who condemn student anarchy most vigorously justify unilateral intervention in the affairs of helpless nations (that is anarchy on an international scale)? And why do those who come down hardest on the law-and-order issue tend to disregard issues of world law and world order?

Lest you misunderstand, I am not advocating irrational violence. I am only trying to explain it and lay open the hypocrisy of our nervous arguments. I happen to believe Berdyaev was right when he said: "Freedom is never achieved by violence, brotherhood through hatred, peace by bloody conflict. Evil means are poisonous. . . . When hatred and revenge are invoked for the sake of liberation, enslavement is the result." [4] But even here, if you defend the American revolution, be willing to extend the argument.

Diana Oughton was born to a family of Middle-American values and wealth. She was educated in the finest schools. After graduating from Bryn Mawr, she worked with the Quakers in Guatemala and in Philadelphia's black ghetto. She was gentle, sensitive, and concerned. But the more she saw and experienced, the more embittered she became. Slowly, even reluctantly, she was radicalized. She moved from a state of ambiguous bitterness into the SDS and its "Jesse James gang" at Ann Arbor. She became a Weatherman. She was in Chicago for the Days of Rage. She went to Cuba. She was arrested in Flint and Chicago. Two perceptive journalists, writing about her, said, "Community organizing had failed. Mass demonstrations had failed. Fighting in the streets had failed. Only terror was left." [5] A gentle, sensitive, deeply concerned girl became a moody, disillusioned revolutionary. She turned to violent terrorism. On March 6, 1970, she and two others were blown to pieces while making bombs in the dingy basement of an old Greenwich Village townhouse. She was destroyed by the violence she had turned to. Don't dismiss her lightly. What had she seen and experienced? What was she rebelling against, and why?

Sometime ago, on the cover of a magazine called *New Left Notes*, there appeared a woodcut illustration of two young men, one white, the other black, crouching on a flaming rooftop. They were urban revolutionaries armed with automatic rifles. Alongside their picture were these words: "We are advocates of the abolition of war, we do not want war; but war can only be abolished through war, and in order to get rid of the gun it is necessary to take up the gun." [6] For the life of me, I fail to see the difference between that "logic" and that of the army major who turned to the war correspondent following the destruction of Ben Tre and said,

"We had to destroy the city in order to save it." Violence begets violence. It is counterproductive. Again, "freedom is never achieved by violence, brotherhood through hatred, peace by bloody conflict."

Christians, whether facing issues of civil disobedience, police brutality, Vietnam, or violent revolutionaries, need to remember that they are called to be peacemakers. To love one's enemies, to pray for one's persecutors, to refuse to retaliate in kind when one is exploited, to try to overcome evil with good, these are the impossible possibilities of the Christian ethic. God was in Christ *reconciling*. The cross, far more eloquently than anything any of us might *say*, reminds us that in the face of hate God loved and gave. When the weapons and strategies of Rome are raised against those who would improve the lot of man, we must remember that those who live by the sword or the rifle or the bomb are invariably involved in their own destruction.

Revolutions deal with styles of life and methods of change. Basically, however, *their characters are determined by their stated purposes and manifestos.*

Most revolutions are bids for freedom. Declaring their independence, our forefathers said, "Whenever any form of government becomes destructive of these ends [man's inalienable rights], it is the right of the people to alter or abolish it." Revolutions are gauntlets thrown at the feet of heartless systems and insensitive rulers. They challenge despotism in the name of the people.

Their manifestos may be utopian or nihilistic. They may spell out the details of a "perfect" order as Karl Marx did in defining his classless society. Or they may call for the random violence and marauding terrorism of faithless despair.

Utopianism, no matter what brand name it bears, is not realistic. It does not take into account man's lust for power, his ugly pride and basic self-centeredness. Nihilism has no point of reference beyond the earthbound and immediate. Its outlook is totally cynical; its defeats are final. Believing in nothing, it has no hope.

The Christian is neither utopian (he knows the painful reality of sin), nor is he a disciple of despair (he believes in God). His revolutionary message, therefore, has a distinctive word for contemporary man.

Acknowledging his self-centered bias, the Christian believes that man is made for community. Community is dependent for its health and stability upon relationship. The laws and institutions of society should reinforce rather than threaten or obstruct relationship. Radical change is required where the possibility for true community is denied. The Christian prays for the divine will to be woven into the life and structures of the world, even as he envisions the coming of a "new earth."

The Christian insists upon the expressed oneness of love and justice. Love without justice is naïve sentimentality. Justice without love is uncompromising legalism. In the ethic of Christ, love and justice are one, and there is no true liberation apart from them.

The Christian takes very seriously the demand for new life in Christ. He is no stranger to radical change. He believes in it. If he is true to the new covenant, he has experienced it. He is a new being. Old things have passed away; all things have become new.

James Smart expressed one of the acute ironies of the present scene when he wrote:

In the first century to be born of the Word and Spirit made Christians revolutionaries who turned the world upside down. How then can 20th century men and women who profess to have been born again be so often the most stubborn opponents of change both in the church and in the social order? [7]

There are Middle-American explanations for the phenomenon, but no *Christian* justification.

The Christian sees true community as an expression of the kingdom of God, love and justice as the requisite for human freedom, and authentic selfhood as the basis of a new humanity. He is not an apologist for any status quo. His is a revolutionary faith; a faith calling for a new style of life in a new kind of world.

The Christian is not a romantic. He knows the harsh realities of struggle and defeat. But he also believes in God! That continuing *act* of faith (and belief is an act, a way of life) makes all the difference. John of Patmos was a political prisoner when he wrote the Revelation. He described the crises of his time with vivid imagery. There were the four horsemen of the apocalypse: conquest, war, famine, and death. There were fire and plagues; natural and cosmic disorders. There were the faithful obedience that led to martyrdom and the faithless betrayal that led to destruction. Sitting atop her seven hills was the "whore of Babylon," the Caesar of Rome, the anti-hero of your choice. When John wrote "God did not forget Babylon the great, but made her drink the cup which was filled with the fierce wine of his vengeance" (Rev. 16:19), he was declaring his independence. He was a revolutionary. He would not bend his knee to Rome. He had been imprisoned by his government for treason. He had put the God of Christ above the rule of Caesar. He was in no mood to repent or recant. He was ultimately answerable to God— and God would speak the final word!

8 Preachers, Churches, and Politics
☆☆☆☆☆☆☆☆☆☆☆☆☆☆

During the 1970 political campaign, the *U.S. News & World Report* featured an article on a new trend: clergymen entering politics. It listed sixteen ministers and priests seeking major offices in the country.[1] Later, Joseph Duffey, a Congregational minister running for the Senate, would be defeated in Connecticut, and Andrew Young, a Baptist preacher, would be upset in his bid for a congressional seat in Atlanta. But in Massachusett's third district, Robert J. Drinan, a Jesuit priest, was elected. His young and ardent supporters carried signs that read: "Our Father who art in Congress." Not many clergymen have been elected. True, the Rev. John Witherspoon, a Presbyterian, signed the Declaration of Independence and served in the Continental Congress, but he set no precedent. Clergymen have been rarities on Capitol Hill. Now, for better or worse, they are becoming increasingly involved in public life.

The current politization of men of the cloth can be traced, in large measure, to the civil rights movement of the 50's and to the clergymen's participation in the peace movement, the black revolution, and efforts on behalf of new social legislation in the 60's. But—and this is an understatement—these clergymen have their criticis. The Roman Catholic hierarchy has frowned on priests' running for public office, and members of every denomination are up in arms. Why? When Thomas Jefferson questioned the right of clergymen to become elected officials, James Madison reminded him of the meaning of freedom of religion. Ministers have civil rights, too. Ordination does not cancel out the privileges and responsibilities of citizenship.

It was long assumed that lawyers, businessmen, educators, and union officials had a right to participate in politics. Now students and welfare mothers are joining the act. Olympic champions and football stars are running for office. The entertainment world has come into its own. George Murphy, recently ousted from his senate seat, is a former song-and-dance man, and Ronald Reagan, of Screen Actors' Guild and class B film fame, is governor of the nation's most populous state. In fact, Governor Reagan was the hottest political property the Republican Party had until Spiro T. Agnew became a household word. Bob Hope, who has studiously avoided partisanship across the years, has become—along with Billy Graham and Arnold Palmer—one of the Nixon Administration's most valuable assets. A *New York Times* reporter, after interviewing Hope, wrote, "He feels that the country is in such a crisis that ordinary rules do not apply." [2] Many of us, though we may not agree with the comedian's opinions on world affairs, agree completely with his sense of urgency.

A political expert in Washington, attempting to explain why clergymen are turning to public life, says, "The war seems to be the major cause. Clergymen are concerned about values and human life. They tend to be idealistic. Clergymen are articulate. They also have a sincere interest in people." [3]

A state legislator in the Upper Midwest was complaining to me some time ago about the political opinions and activities of ministers in his state. "After all," he said, "they haven't had any experience. They don't know anything about politics."

I asked him what his experience had been before he ran for state office. "I was a businessman," he said.

"What business were you in?"

A bit self-consciously he confessed that he had run a children's train at an entertainment park. When you take into consideration a clergyman's concern for people, his ethical commitments, and his academic training, maybe his credentials are not so inferior after all.

Quite apart from a churchman's decision to run for office are other deeper considerations. What are we to think when the World Council of Churches devotes much of the agenda at its Fourth Assembly to the plight of underdeveloped nations? What about a church group giving money to the Angela Davis defense fund? What about the Fundamentalist radio preacher, Carl McIntire, conducting "win the war" rallies all over the place, and Jesse Jackson wielding black power in the Illinois State Legislature? What about church leaders and groups coming out for or against the bussing of school children, for or against open housing and fair employment laws, for or against censorship or abortion, for or against the legalization of marijuana? How can the church justify its increasing involvement in things secular and controversial?

Like it or not, the Bible seems to be on the side of the "meddling" activists. Think of the people: Joseph, the pharaoh's prime minister; Moses, the revolutionary; Deborah, a combination of Joan of Arc and Bernadette Devlin; Samuel, the circuit court judge setting the stage for a united kingdom. There were the prophets, the disturbers of the peace: Elijah, defying a queen; Nathan, shaming a king; Isaiah, warning and counseling an assortment of rulers; Hosea, denouncing the princes and courts of his land; and Amos, thundering the judgments of God down upon the greed and insensitivity of his people.

At the center of the biblical revelation stands Jesus of Nazareth, who began his public career by announcing his special ministry to the poor, the blind, and the captive, and who, three years later, was dead, killed by the vested interests of both church and state because of his subversive influence among the faithful. "They say you are King of the Jews," they charged. "Are you King of the Jews?" they asked. His answers were not satisfactory. They killed the troublemaker.

When clerics speak out against government policy in Southeast Asia, or the military/industrial complex, or the irresponsible rhetoric of politicians, their pious critics often quote the man from Nazareth: "Render unto Caesar the things that are Caesar's and unto God the things that are God's." Those who quote Jesus forget two things. They forget that one of the reasons Jesus was put to death was because he was considered a threat to the Caesar. And they don't think through the phrase "render unto God the things that are God's." What belongs to God? I belong to God. You belong to God. Our children and our children's children belong to God. This good earth belongs to God. And *anything* that defaces or destroys this earth and its inhabitants is the business of free and conscientious men.

This is why the church, if it is faithful to its biblical roots, will be concerned about people (all sorts and conditions of people) and will deal with those issues that are central to the human story.

If faithful, the church will become involved in the struggles of the black man, Mexican-American, red man, and Puerto Rican. This means more than observing Race Relations Sunday, sending an annual donation to the NAACP, or serving on the Board of the Urban League. It means doing our homework—taking the Kerner Report more seriously than Washington did; studying the plight of farm workers in California and the style of leadership provided by Cesar Chavez; coming to grips with the pathos, the virtual hopelessness, that gives birth to revolutionary Black Panther and Young Lord organizations. What does Vine Deloria say about the American Indian? What do Julian Bond and Ralph Abernathy say about the black man? More important, what are our churches *learning* about the battered and disinherited? And what are our churches *doing?*

If faithful to its biblical roots, the church will be concerned about personal morality. It will refuse to be considered square when it questions the tragic meaninglessness of the deaths of Jimi Hendrix and Janis Joplin. It will take seriously the question Senator Hughes is asking: "Are we an intoxicated nation?" Some fifteen million young Americans are smoking marijuana. There are hundreds of thousands of heroin addicts in the country. (The current urban crime wave is directly related to drug addiction.) We are taking pills for everything—even when the Pope tells us not to. Eighty-five million Americans consume alcoholic beverages and more than 10 percent of that number are considered problem drinkers. A dangerous dependence upon drugs is emerging as a style of life for the bored, defeated, and rebellious. I quite agree with those who say the counter culture has much to teach us, but the counter culture is a "mixed bag." Its amoral sexuality and its ambivalence toward hard drugs threaten both the well-being of persons and the delicate fabric of true community.

If faithful to its biblical roots, the church will be concerned about preserving man's environment. We have explored and cultivated this good earth, probing its mysteries, harnessing its energies, and subjugating its resources. But while mastering our surroundings, we have dangerously defiled them. We have scarred this earth's natural beauty, polluted its water and air, and stripped it of irreplaceable wealth. Expanding population, industrialization, carelessness, and greed have combined to threaten the planet's capacity to support human life.

God created the earth and called it good. If its life and health are threatened, this becomes the churches' business.

The number one issue of our time is: the survival of man in a world of irrational violence. If the church is faithful to its biblical roots, it will not turn away from One who said, "Blessed are the peacemakers," and who warned that those who live by the sword will, by that same sword, die. Think—

An arms race continues virtually unchecked as we approach a nuclear Armageddon. Even as SALT talks go on, MIRV is deployed, and the lethal competition reaches another deadly plateau.

A military/industrial complex controls our destinies far more than any of us realize. More than six thousand public relations men work for the Pentagon, helping convince the American taxpayer that he is justified in supporting some two thousand military bases around the world. The hidden budget of this selling job approaches $200 million a year.

The war in Southeast Asia grinds on. Hundreds of thousands of Vietnamese people are dead; one of four in South Vietnam is displaced. Cambodia has burst into flames, because we decided to "protect our boys" in yet one more country. Laos is invaded by our "freedom-loving" allies from Saigon, as we pound it from the air.

An Old Testament prophet once foresaw the coming of a day when justice would flow down upon the children of this earth as waters, and righteousness as a mighty stream. Until that day comes, the churches and their spokesmen must continue to seek justice, goodness, freedom, and peace, even when vigorously opposed and frightfully misunderstood.

But how? How can Christians relate the lives of their churches to the urgency of the hour? How can we best influence the processes of history during these fateful 1970's?

We can try to speak the truth. (That has always been the church's long suit.) But talk, though necessary, can be totally irrelevant. To put one's body on the line is something else again. That is what Martin Luther King did. That is what Paul Moore, tall, lean, artistocratic bishop of the Protestant Episcopal Church, did in June of 1970 when he went to Saigon and marched with Vietnamese students in protest against the war and the Thieu-Ky police state. The direct involvement of the marcher, protester, or dissenter is one way of challenging the course of history.

There is also partisan political action. Robert McAfee Brown wrote an open letter to Vice-President Agnew (before the Vice-President simmered down following the '70 elections) that represented partisan criticism at its best. He wrote as a "parent of sons of draft age," as a university professor, as a clergyman, and as an American. He wrote, "Mr. Agnew: . . . You have indeed won instant fame, but at a price—a price higher for the nation than for yourself: the phenomenon of a Vice-President spreading fear and invective across the land reflects a country being urged by its elected leadership to abandon thought and rationality at a time when we have special need of the ability to understand one another rather than to hate." [4] That sort of partisanship is not only legitimate, but necessary.

Sometimes, of course, our activism will be resented and misunderstood. In October of 1970, I flew into Indianapolis, where I had served for ten years, to speak at a statewide luncheon for Vance Hartke. Senator Hartke has long been challenging our policies in Southeast Asia, and his voting record on Capitol Hill coincides with the emphases of the social creed of the church I seek to serve. He was being challenged by a "superhawk." If the political process is important, and if that process is designed to cope with the most urgent issues of the day, if we are a government of laws and not of men, then it becomes necessary to speak out and become involved even when there are risks to be run. Some of the mail I received following that Indianapolis appearance was hostile beyond belief, but Hartke squeaked through, and I had the satisfaction of knowing that, in a very small way, I had contributed to the victory. Although the church, as *such,* cannot become the tool of partisanship or the voice of particular candidates for public office, there will be those within it, both laymen and clergymen, who will express their Christian idealism and indignation in partisan ways.

Some will engage in lobbying. James Adams, in his recent book *The Growing Church Lobby in Washington,* documents the lobbying activities of certain religious groups and organizations. He pays special attention to the church's role in the development and passage of civil rights legislation. More recently the church has been dramatically involved in lobbying for specific peace legislation on Capitol Hill. The Roman Catholic Church has been active in fighting for parochial school aid and against more liberal abortion laws.

But lawmaking is only a part of it. There is no substitute for the life well lived. Christianity is incarnational. As Oppenheimer once said, "The best way to send an idea is to wrap it up in a person." Beyond the spoken word and the specific political action taken is the gift of life itself.

"Greater love hath no man than this, that a man lay down his life for his friends." We have seen the brothers Kennedy die as political martyrs in our time. We have seen Dietrich Bonhoeffer and Martin Luther King die as religious martyrs. Our sacrifice will not be the same. But, bit by bit, day by day, we are called to offer ourselves on behalf of the broken and defenseless. This overall commitment should give shape to the disciplines we accept for ourselves, our styles of life, our vocational choices, our idealism and political stance, and should help us better understand why other people function as they do in the name and grace of their convictions.

9 The Ecology Kick
☆ ☆ ☆ ☆ ☆ ☆ ☆

For thousands of years religious seers and alarmists have talked about an end time. Maybe this is it.

There is the population explosion. Julius Caesar's world was inhabited by 150 million people. We add that many to the world's population every two years. If our present rate of growth continues, Paul Ehrlich warns, in less than a thousand years, sixty million billion people will live on this planet; that is one hundred people for every square yard of the earth's surface.[1]

There is racism. A fierce racial self-consciousness has supplanted earlier and more palatable melting-pot ideals designed to refashion minority groups in the dominant image of the majority. If the black man, the red man, the Mexican-American, the cultural and racial outsider is not soon given his legitimate piece of the action, blood is certain to run red.

There is poverty. One out of three people in this land of affluence is poor. Our unemployment rate is the highest in a decade. It is a prohibitive 9 percent among our black brothers. If this nation with its unbelievable economic and natural resources is unwilling to share those resources equitably with all its people, then again the stage is set for the violent rejection of the status quo.

This address was delivered on January 14, 1971, at Oklahoma City University's Mid-Year Institute. The theme of the Institute was "Man and His Precarious Environment."

Victims of poverty and racial injustice in America consider themselves aligned with the poor and the "put-upon" everywhere. They have identified with the Third World and are no longer willing to submit to the plans and the whims of the powerful.

There is the threat of global destruction: the absolute certainty of a nuclear and biochemical holocaust unless the wills of militarists, industrialists, technocrats, and bureaucrats, are made subservient to the common good.

Critics of the so-called ecology kick argue that the new interest in environment is a cop-out, a smoke screen designed to obscure the more pressing and controversial issues of war, economics, and race. They say that science and technology will provide. We can distill ocean water, utilize hybrid grains and fertilizers, colonize other planets, harness atomic energy, and subdue the earth. Nature is ours to conquer, they say. This, of course, is a part of the problem. Does this earth exist for the sake of man alone? Do we have a right to defile and reconstruct the created order? What of the delicate balance of nature, the mystical web of life? What are we presently doing to upset that balance and rip apart the web?

Our air is being poisoned; our water is being polluted; our land is being raped.

I did much of my growing up in Southern California, with its mountains, deserts, orange groves, vineyards, and beaches. Today the mountains are burned brown, the groves and vineyards are being crowded out, the ocean is fouled with oil and sewage, the landscape is cluttered with ticky-tack houses, huge billboards, neon signs, and intricate geometric patterns of concrete, where cars and trucks fill the air with carbon monoxide and diesel fumes while inching forward six abreast for miles on end. As far as one can see—and it isn't very far these days—the dirty air hangs heavy through the valleys. When landing at the Los Angeles airport, you brace yourself to bounce off the smog as you make your reentry. What is said of Los Angeles can be said of other urban concentrations across this land.

Internal-combustion motors are the chief offenders, but they have been joined by electrical and nuclear power plants, jet-powered engines, and an assortment of monuments to our technological prowess.

Flagstaff, Arizona, was once considered the last outpost of clean, pure air in the country, but six years ago clouds of pollution from Southern California drifted eastward to change all that. Today, power plants built in New Mexico and Arizona to feed the insatiable industrial appetite of Southern California fill the air with refuse. Pollution has become indigenous to the wide open spaces of the great Southwest.

The Colorado River, which originates as a sweet mountain stream north of Denver, carries more than a ton of salt per acre-foot as it approaches the Mexican border. Some parts of the Ohio River have zero oxygen. The Potomac is a moving cesspool. More than 11,000 miles of our rivers and streams have been severely damaged by acid drainage.

Lake Erie is virtually dead. Lake Michigan is critically sick. Even the seven seas are being threatened as never before. The author of *The Biological Time Bomb* says, "The oceans are filling up with junk and assorted poisons." He goes on to say that we are dumping "oil, chemical effluents, heavy metals, . . . dry-cleaning fluids, radioactive wastes, chemical warfare gases and irritants, detergents, pesticides, and innumerable other substances"[2] into the waters of the sea. Some 500,000 tons of crude oil—leaked or deliberately dumped—pollute the oceans every year. Marine scientists predict that, if we continue to use the sea as a global trash can, marine life could be destroyed within fifty years.

The sea is not our only trash can. The land is cluttered now with heaps of cans and cars, bottles and jars, garbage and sewage (less than one-third of the people in this country are served by adequate sewage-disposal systems); highways and parking lots are bulldozing people out of the way; forests are being leveled, and the precious soil of earth is being threatened by science. Last year more than one billion pounds of pesticides were used on our gardens, lawns, farms, and forests. There is a 14 percent increase in the use of pesticides every year, and we don't even know what is poison and what is not.

A few months ago I shared in the Congressional Conference on War and National Responsibility and heard Arthur Galston, professor of biology at Yale, argue that we are not committing genocide on the people of Vietnam; that is, despite appearances we are not trying to destroy an entire people. But we are committing ecocide; that is, with the systematic and massive use of scientific technology we are destroying the environment of a people. Since 1962, C-123 cargo planes have released more than 100 million pounds of herbicides over more than 4 million acres of land. Recently the American Association for the Advancement of Science charged that one-fifth of the 1,200,000 acres of mangrove forests in South Vietnam have been utterly destroyed by defoliants.

Ecocide may result from conscious strategy, as in Vietnam, or unconscious bungling, as in parts of China, Russia, and the United States, but its end result, its impact upon nature's balance, will be the same.

The environmental crisis has been produced by an American value system that has deified industrial growth and technological development. Barry Weisberg, writing about the oil industry's designs upon Alaska, says:

Domination through growth has mesmerized the American mind for so long that the suggestion of curtailing growth is unthinkable. Greek rationalism, the Roman engineering mentality, the biblical injunction to conquer and subdue nature, the post-Enlightenment mystique about technical progress—all espouse development. . . . Yet, the old myth that continued growth increases our control over the environment is now simply false. We are losing control. We are destroying the air we breathe, the water we drink and the land we walk on.[3]

Congress has passed some fifty laws related to our environment since 1945; nearly half of them since 1963. The Nixon Administration has made a point of declaring war on pollution. But the fact remains that government agencies, the Corps of Engineers, the Atomic Energy Commission, TVA, and others, are among the chief offenders of the land. As Senator Gaylord Nelson has said, "The leadership of the country has brought little more than cosmetic rhetoric to the environment crisis." [4]

I come to you as a churchman. I have been asked to deal with the moral and ethical implications of the crisis. What does the religious conscience say in the presence of the threatened destruction of this good earth? Almost anything you want it to say.

There are those who argue, as did Barry Weisberg, that the religious community is a part of the problem. A recent manual on ecology and politics charges, quite rightly, I fear, that "Christianity has indirectly assisted in the creation of a social indifference to nature and to the development of a world view which sees man as somehow apart from and not subject to the web of biological interdependencies which finally sustain all life." [5]

A young Christian scholar, Frederick Elder, has written an extremely helpful study of man and his environment.[6] In it he talks about "exclusionists" and "inclusionists." Exclusionists are those who would exclude man from the natural domain, insisting that man is superior to the created order and is entitled to subdue it. Inclusionists, on the other hand, see themselves as an integral part of the created order and affirm an almost mystical identification with every form of life.

Included among the exclusionists are no lesser lights than the late Jesuit priest and paleontologist Pierre Teilhard de Chardin and the brilliant, provocative Harvard scholar Harvey Cox. They insist that man is the center of everything, that he has been given dominion over everything, and that he will either eliminate or subject to his control every nonhuman biological form and expression.[7]

To act upon this faith will lead, eventually, to the creation of an artificial environment or to the total elimination of a life-supporting environment. *Technocracy and megapolis can so intrude upon the delicate balance of nature as to destroy it and us together.*

The most eloquent inclusionist is Loren Eiseley, anthropologist, naturalist, and teacher of man. Eiseley accepts man's unique capacities. He finds, however, "mystery in the heart of a simple seed," [8] and insists that man and nature are bound together in the "miracle" of transcendent reality. Wonder and reverence mark Eiseley's posture in the presence of all creation.

Forgetting labels for the moment, let me try to define our situation. There is no way we can turn the clock back. There is no way to erase from the story of mankind the industrial revolution, technology, urbanization, the unbelievable fruits of modern science, and now, the promise of a nuclear age. We can no more return to the village and the spinning wheel than could Mohandas Gandhi. The machine, with all its latter-day developments, is with us and will continue with us.

But—and this is at the heart of the argument—man, by limiting his destiny to that of the machine, can become a machine, a robot, an automaton. He can be dehumanized. Or, man can understand that he has emerged from nature and that his destiny is inseparably linked with that of nature.

It is neither necessary nor inevitable that we be destroyed by the limitations, the finiteness, the arrogance of a mechanized humanity.

In a word: *Either we will use the remarkable advances of the past century to preserve our natural environment, or by destroying our environment we will write the last chapter of man's history on this earth.*

What can we do to preserve our environment?

We can begin by affirming the oneness, the wholeness, of creation. Back in 1964, Rachel Carson, who was saying the essential word long before it had occurred to most of us, referred to "a complex, precise and highly integrated system of relationships between living things which cannot be safely ignored any more than the law of gravity can be defied with impunity." [9] Barry Commoner has been even more specific.

We have come to the turning point in the human habitation of the earth. The environment is a complex, subtly balanced system, and it is this integrated whole which receives the impact of all separate insults inflicted by pollutants. . . . I believe that the cumulative effects of these pollutants, their interactions and amplifications, can be fatal to the complex fabric of the biosphere. [10]

A Greek philosopher once said, "If you kick a stone you jar the universe." By the same token, if you intrude upon or infect any part of the natural order, you affect it all. The ecosystems of this planet are wondrously interrelated and require the maintenance of an essential balance if the web of life is to be preserved.

We can begin by affirming the oneness, the wholeness of creation. If that is our point of beginning, then we are called to assume personal responsibility for keeping the whole intact.

This means an awareness of little things: lighting matches in dry wooded areas; carelessly discarding refuse; dumping junk in waterways and open spaces. I remember, as a teen-ager, working in a warehouse at an Army Air Depot. One day I finished my work, got on a bus, ate a candy bar, and threw the wrapper out a window. An executive type sitting next to me looked disdainfully at me and told me not to clutter up the premises. I resented it at the time. Who did he think he was? Just because I was a dirty kid in work clothes. Yet as I look back, that was my first important lesson in environ-mental control. As Pogo says, "We have met the enemy and he is us."

As consumers in the world's most affluent society, we need to place restraints upon ourselves. We do not need to eat as much as we eat, drive the high-powered cars we drive, use the electricity we use, enter into the patterns of waste that have become characteristic of our kind. As Jean Mayer said in a recent interview, "It's the rich who wreck the environment. Rich people occupy more space, consume more of each natural resource, disturb the ecology more, litter the land-scape with bottles and papers, and pollute more land, air and water with chemical, thermal and radioactive waste." [11] Mayer went on to say that if China, with its 700 million people, was as wealthy as the United States it would be wrecked in no time. "It is the spread of wealth that threatens the environ-ment, just as it is the spread of fat that threatens the lives of so many Americans." [12] We must assume full responsibility for the good fortune that is ours.

An ethic of ecology will not only accept personal respon-sibility, but also accept and encourage essential social and economic change. No economic system, no dedication to industrial growth and technological progress, no quest for profit, comfort, or security dare be permitted to destroy man's habitat. We cannot expect industry to regulate in-dustry. As long as major polluters dominate our antipollution boards and profiteers with major vested interests are selected to police environmental reform, there is little hope.

The chairman of Standard Oil of Indiana says, "The central question is not whether we should have cleaner water, but how clean, at what cost. . . . Public enthusiasm for pollution control is matched by reluctance to pay even a modest share of the cost. This attitude will have to change." [13] A lot of attitudes will have to change: the attitude of the public *and* the attitude of Standard Oil! Government agencies, public utilities, and private companies must be judged on the basis of their relationship to people and their environment. We do not exist to make men wealthy; the wealth of this earth exists to sustain and ennoble life.

All this suggests that our active participation is needed in the political processes of municipality, state, and nation. Support Mr. Nixon when he implements his splendid rhetoric with action. Support Senators Muskie, Nelson, Proxmire, McGovern, Hart, and Case when they sponsor legislation designed to protect the environment against unreasonable impairment. Yes, and when it becomes obvious that your congressmen have sold out to those who are despoiling this good earth, challenge and oppose them.

Some action groups you may identify with are:

Sierra Club
1050 Mills Tower
San Francisco, California 94104

Center for the Study of Responsive Law
1908 Q Street N.W.
Washington, D.C. 20009

Ralph Nader's incredibly effective efforts.

Friends of the Earth
30 East 42nd Street
New York, New York 10017

Zero Population Growth
330 Second Street
Los Altos, California 94022

Environmental Action
2000 P Street N.W.
Washington, D.C. 20036

Conservation and education groups include:

International Union for Conservation of Nature and
Natural Resources
2000 P Street N.W.
Washington, D.C. 20006

The Izaak Walton League of America
1326 Waukegan Road
Glenview, Illinois 60025

John Muir Institute for Environmental Studies
451 Pacific Avenue
San Francisco, California 94133
Or: P.O. Box 11
Cedar Crest, New Mexico 87008

Citizens League Against the Sonic Boom
19 Appleton Street
Cowbridge, Massachusetts 02138

Planned Parenthood/World Population
515 Madison Avenue
New York, New York 10022

Scientists' Institute for Public Information
30 E. 68th Street
New York, New York 10021

The Nature Conservancy
1522 K Street N.W.
Washington, D.C. 2005

The National Wildlife Federation
1412 16th Street N.W.
Washington, D.C. 20036

National Audubon Society
1130 Fifth Avenue
New York, New York 10028

The Conservation Foundation
1250 Connecticut Avenue N.W.
Washington, D.C. 20036

The Wilderness Society
729 15th Street N.W.
Washington, D.C. 20005

National Parks Association
1701 18th Street N.W.
Washington, D.C. 20009

The "ecology kick" is just that; a sudden, soaring thrust of environmental concern. It is a bandwagon. Get on board! Alarmists insist it is already too late. Perhaps not. That may well depend upon people like us. Henry Thoreau's pond, Albert Schweitzer's "reverence for life," Rachel Carson's "silent spring," and Loren Eiseley's "immense journey" have so much to teach us.

The sacred scriptures of the Judeo-Christian tradition begin with the words: "In the beginning God created the heavens and the earth . . . and He said, 'That is good.' " Let's keep it that way.

10 Is Peace a Dirty Word?
☆ ☆ ☆ ☆ ☆ ☆ ☆ ☆ ☆ ☆

There is much talk today about polarization; about generational conflict and a communications gap. So what's new? Centuries ago Jesus not only predicted, but also assumed responsibility for such rifts between us. "I didn't come to make things peaceful," he said, "but to bring division; to pit sons against fathers, mothers against daughters, one generation against another." Speaking to people who should have had deeper insight, he said, "You fools! Why can't you interpret this fateful hour?" (See Luke 12:49-56.)

That was a fateful hour. So is this! Our environment is being destroyed. Population is exploding. Hunger is everywhere. People, long-oppressed, are demanding their rights, and are being goaded into violence. And there is war—the threat of all-out nuclear war and the insanity of particular brush-fire wars. For instance, nothing is dividing North American people more than the war in Vietnam.

Oh, the rhetoric of peace is plentiful. Everybody pays lip service to peace: East/West; Hanoi/Saigon; New Left/Radical Right; five-star-general/conscientious objector; George Wallace as well as William Fulbright; Carl McIntire as well as William Sloan Coffin. We are all for peace—in the abstract.

This sermon was preached on April 22, 1970, to The General Conference of The United Methodist Church in St. Louis, Missouri. Since then more than 75,000 copies have been circulated by the Board of Christian Social Concerns.

It is the particularities, the specifics, that divide us. It is precisely here, in dealing with specifics, that man's survival will be made possible or his destruction inevitable.

Some of those who talk grandiloquently about peace in general seem to regard it as a dirty word when its advocates critically evaluate the specifics of national policy in its name. In a climate of crisis the chauvinist often insists that peace and patriotism are anthithetical terms. When convinced idealists apply the imperatives of peace to Southeast Asia or the Pentagon or the military/industrial complex, "peace" becomes a dirty word, seeming to indicate weakness, spinelessness, cowardice, treason.

I would remind you of the obvious: We are not primarily Americans—or citizens of any nation—but Christians. The Pentagon is *not* our national cathedral; Mars is *not* our God. We are those (in theory at least) who seek first God's kingdom and move under the lordship of Christ.

For us peace is not a plank on a political platform or the fervent hope of the administration of our choice. It is a tenet of the faith; an imperative of the gospel. It follows that a *militarized* society, whether it is here or in Greece or Russia or Latin America, denies the gospel and is a foe of the faith.

What is a militarized society? Donald McDonald, in a recent essay, insists it is an *authoritarian* society in which dissent cannot be tolerated. It is a society that puts *stability* above all else, considering law and order more important than justice and human rights. It is a *fearful* society, a *self-righteous* society, a *sterile* society (in which "effete intellectual snobs" are considered traitors).[1]

Then McDonald zeros in on the brass and the braids of it all.

The militarized society makes an unchallengeable claim on the lives of its young. That is what the draft—compulsory conscription—is all about.

The militarized society is beyond effective criticism and control. Far more than one-half the budget of the United States is related to wars—past, present, and future. This part of the budget is beyond the effective reach of checks, balances, and civilian control. It is like a virgin maiden, not to be looked at too closely, not to be touched, certainly not to be violated.

Deception is accepted as a normal fact of life in a militarized society. (The Pentagon Papers have dramatically underscored the roles of manipulation and deceit in the formation of public policy.) Do you remember the U-2 incident, the Bay of Pigs, the Bay of Tonkin? Now it's Cambodia and Laos. Deceit: Is there a better word to describe it when secrecy and distortion or denial of fact join to justify public policy?

The militarized society sees political problems in military terms and seeks military solutions for them. We have downgraded the Paris peace talks while putting all our eggs in the basket of Vietnamization. We have thus downgraded the political solution while turning, once again, to the military. One of the places where the Paris negotiations are hung up is at the point of the "representative" nature of the Thieu-Ky government. We are not willing to admit that the present Saigon regime is a corrupt military police state, defying the processes and options of true self-determination while clinging to power.

We can rejoice in President Nixon's announced goal of returning another 150,000 troops to their American homeland, but are we willing to face the unpleasant fact that, in the process, we are transferring military hardware into the hands of the Saigon generals, leaving 80 percent of the people—most of them Buddhist peasants who don't have the slightest idea of what the war is all about—caught in a crossfire between Communist terrorism on the one hand and police-state oppression on the other? When will we learn that bullets, bombs, and herbicides will not defeat communism in Asia; only the *people* of Asia can do that as they respond to a demonstrably better way.

Again, *in a militarized society the economy is dependent upon the military.* Do you realize that one out of nine jobs in the United States is related to the Department of Defense? That we maintain 340 major military bases and 1,930 minor bases around the world at a cost of $5 billion a year? And we have already said it, far more than half our national budget is related to the military.

To summarize: *The military claims the highest priority in a militarized society.* The book *American Militarism: 1970,* an outgrowth of the Congressional Conference on Military Budget and National Priorities, opens with the words:

Our country is in danger of becoming a national security state. Since the end of World War II we have spent more than one trillion dollars, or two-thirds of the total expenditures of our federal government, on armaments and armed forces. Today, almost eighty percent of our federal appropriations are allocated to defense and defense-related costs.[2]

Richard Barnet, a former State Department official, is far more pointed when he bluntly insists that "the central activity" of our government is "planning and carrying out wars."[3]

Don't you see, when you talk about peace in these terms, attacking a war psychology, a war economy, a *war system,* then peace becomes a dirty word in some very respectable circles. But how else can we talk about peace with meaning? Unless we talk about it in context, specifically, without equivocation or apology, we will never be in a position to beat our swords into plowshares or our thermonuclear warheads into power plants for peace. Our apathetic silence, or our shared caution and cowardice, may well permit life on this planet to be swallowed up in death.

It is not easy to stand up for peace in our kind of world. We are surrounded by masses who do not, who *will* not understand the signs of the times. They do not comprehend the fatefulness of this hour.

On February 12, 1970, newspapers across the land carried two stories. One dealt with one of Vice-President Agnew's purple invective speeches. He had caricatured young war protesters and said he would "like to swap the whole damn zoo [of young dissenters] for a single platoon of the kind of young Americans" he had seen in Vietnam. The other article told about the death of one of those young Americans, a GI named Danny Ray Roberts. From Vietnam, Roberts had sent a sealed envelope to his Tennessee home, asking that it be opened in the event of his death. On February 4, he was killed. His letter was opened. In it he said, "I died needlessly, along with a lot of my comrades." Fine young Americans in Vietnam are as concerned about the war as fine young Americans in the United States.

Lieutenant Louis Fort is a twenty-four-year-old United Methodist and West Point graduate. After what he called agonizing study and meditation, he refused to go to Vietnam. "The war in Vietnam is immoral and unjust," he wrote. "The My Lai incident strongly crystallized my belief."

"I love my God and my country," he said, "but I love my God first." There you have it!

Nor are we simply dealing with the politics, psychology, and economics of war. We are talking about humanity. We are talking about *survival*. G. Lowe Dickinson said it for me: "My theme may be put in a sentence," he wrote. "If mankind does not end war, war will end mankind." We are not cave-

men with clubs in our hands, but we may prove to be cave-
men with ABM and MIRV at our disposal.

We have a son-in-law who is still in college. Sometime ago
he wrote about the backwash of the bomb:

> Little tree—
> Your tortured limbs and yellowed
>   leaves are the last signs of life.
> Hold me—
> Too weak to stand, too crippled
>   to lie; tree, support me as
>   my last breath passes.
> Was it all a dream?
> Tell me, bush, did smiling faces,
>   noisy streets, quiet parks
>   ever exist?
> Is nothing as it seems?
> Dust and ashes now pile where
>   I thought my sister was
>   sleeping in the grass.
> It's us alone.
> Are we alone? Have years of
>   work and meaning come to
>   this—disintegration?
> Lord, make yourself known!
> Tree, answer please. Where have
>   they put Him; what has
>   become of Him?
> *Where is God? . . .* [4]

Where is God? God was and *is* in Christ, *reconciling.*
Christ's coming was heralded with words "peace on earth."
Do we believe that is what he came to bring? How? Through
whom?

The Christ of God said, "Love God with all your energies and resources, and love one another." That is our point of beginning.

He said, "Love your enemies. Pray for those who persecute and despitefully use you." He must have understood that good will ultimately overcome evil, and that today's enemies are tomorrow's friends; that enemies are manufactured and defined by those who need them to justify their own violent hostility.

He said, "Those who live by the sword will perish by the sword." Today we are told that we can overkill the Russians about 160 times; they can kill each of us only about 100 times. This gives us an extremely reassuring advantage! Dear friends, those who live by the bomb will perish by the bomb. We reap what we sow.

And Jesus said, "Blessed are the peacemakers, for they shall be called the children of God." Do we who name his name *really* believe that?

We do not have to accept the ethical imperatives of the new covenant if we don't want to. If we choose to reject love and justice and peace, well and good. We have the right. But we must bear in mind what else and Who else we are rejecting in the process.

If peace is a dirty word, then Christ was a dirty liar and history is a dirty joke; life is a cruel wasteland, and violence and hate have license to prevail.

No! This we do *not* believe. We are Christians, and we have been raised up for such a time as this. We believe in God. As we are faithful and obedient, God will be with us, believing in us, empowering us, enabling us to join him in extending the boundaries of his kingdom in his world, that just peace might reign and his will might be done, on earth in history even as it is beyond.

Myths and Madness 11
☆ ☆ ☆ ☆ ☆ ☆ ☆ ☆ ☆

I once heard Charles Wells, of *Between the Lines,* say that the only good thing he could see coming out of the war in Vietnam was its revelation of the futility and duplicity of modern warfare. The news media have brought its irony and tragedy into our homes, and there is no way to escape the implications of credibility gaps and two-sided questions. Following the Cambodian "incursion" and Kent State's reaction, a single NBC news report contained several conversational segments. First, there was an interview with National Guardsmen who had been on the Kent State campus. They showed no remorse for the killing of the four students; only a sense of frustrated anger. Then there were interviews with GI's in Cambodia. They did not want to be there. They were dirty and tired, and even as the correspondent talked with them, a burst of enemy fire forced them to hit the ground and take cover. Finally, there was a conversation with the parents of one of the girls killed by troops at Kent State. The father, a well-dressed executive type, said he could not believe this was America. Nazi Germany perhaps, Russia perhaps, but not America. Nearly a year later, cameras and correspondents would combine to indict the "logic" and rhetoric surrounding the Laotian "incursion." It is hard for people to deny what they see and hear, and a press corps (though sometimes muzzled) has helped us see and hear unfolding events as no other people have been enabled to observe them.

95

Noam Chomsky, long a critic of our Asian policy, has said, "The course of history may be determined . . . by what the people of the United States will have learned from this catastrophe." [1] "This catastrophe," of course, refers to Indochina. Just as Great Britain "lost its virginity" during the Boer War and in Gandhi's India, just as Germany did the same under Hitler and France to the Viet Minh and in Algeria, so now we, as a nation, have discovered we can be wrong, too. Or have we?

Southeast Asia has exposed the costly error of a wide assortment of American opinions, presuppositions, and policies. It has exposed the madness of some of our favorite myths.

To begin, there is the pervading and ominous myth that *there is no such thing as a military/industrial complex in the United States.* Militarists argue that only naïve do-gooders and paranoid alarmists are concerned. For the sake of the future, I hope concern is not limited to the nervous and naïve. Human survival is at stake.

The military/industrial complex began to assume its present form during World War II. After decades of mutual suspicion, business and the armed services were forced together. After the war they continued to pursue their mutual interests. Their growing power caused President Eisenhower, as he left office, to warn against their dominance in public life. Ironically, it was John Kennedy, trying to assert civilian control over the military, who tipped the scales in the opposite direction. He named Robert McNamara his Secretary of Defense. McNamara, with rare wizardry, brought the various branches of the armed services together, encouraged greater intimacy between business and the military, and enthroned the computer as god of all operational procedure. Never had the military life of the nation been so efficiently organized. But, even here, the expanding war in Southeast Asia brought unforeseen consequences. David Halberstam, in a brilliant study of McNamara, writes:

As the war destroyed the domestic programs of Lyndon Johnson and drove him out of office, it similarly destroyed what McNamara had done at the Pentagon. . . . He had chosen above all else to *control* the Pentagon, and with the war he had lost control of the machinery. . . . Rather than being a Defense Secretary for seven years, a case could be made that he was really only in charge four. He spent his time and his resources trying to hold the generals back." [2]

With the invasion of Cambodia and Laos, as well as a resumption of bombing in North Vietnam, it would appear that the Nixon Administration heeded the Joint Chiefs of Staff even more than its predecessor. Anthony Lewis, trying to explain student anger following Cambodia, said, "They see, despite elections and changes of government, the undiminished power of the military." [3]

Today the military/industrial complex consists of competing branches of the armed services which exaggerate real or imagined external threats to this country in order to justify astronomical "defense" appropriations; militarized civilians—businessmen, lawyers, and an assortment of bureaucrats who find their professional stance and direction within the framework of a war psychology and economy; of "defense" contractors—like Lockheed—who are pampered and subsidized by the government (giving rise to the phrase "military socialism"); and a sprawling public relations apparatus designed to brainwash Congress and the citizenry alike. CBS, with its controversial documentary "The Selling of the Pentagon," simply revealed dangerous truths that officials had tried to keep hidden from the people they are theoretically called to serve.

A trillion and a half dollars have been spent on our warmaking machinery since 1945. More than half our tax dollars go for past, present, and future wars. According to Arthur Burns, chairman of the Federal Reserve Board, the "true military budget" for 1971, including tangential costs, was more than $106 billion.[4] We are now told that, even if we leave Vietnam tomorrow, new weapons systems will require a continuation of present rates of spending. The fact that F. Edward Hebert has replaced Mendel Rivers as chairman of the powerful House Armed Services Committee has not changed a thing. The old "Rivers' Law" seems to prevail. It goes something like this: The military cannot survive unless it prospers, it cannot prosper unless it grows, and it cannot grow if it permits itself to be blocked by any logic not its own.

How does this relate to Indochina? John Kenneth Galbraith has said, "We shall have accomplished little if we get out of Vietnam and leave uncontrolled the influences that were responsible for the disaster, for the Bay of Pigs and for the Dominican Republic." Significantly, he went on to say, "We can't have a crusade against military men as such. Indeed, our purpose is to restore the military profession to its historic and honored role." [5] Historically, the military has served the purposes of the citizen in the United States. More and more, those roles have been reversed. There *is* a pervasive military/industrial complex in this country, misleading and dangerous myths to the contrary.

Another myth, *we say we are in Southeast Asia as the champions of freedom.* We justify our presence there by referring to SEATO (Southeast Asia Treaty Organization) agreements and guarantees. But where did SEATO come from? It was the creation of John Foster Dulles, designed to legitimatize our presence in Vietnam. Signatories included only three Asian countries: the Philippines (a former American colony),

Thailand (a client state) and Pakistan (which has since withheld both support and sympathy from our Vietnamese folly). Mr. Dulles once said, "SEATO's *principal* purpose was to provide our president *legal* authority to intervene in Indochina." [6] Our intentions were so transparent (the SEATO conference was held in Manila just a month after Geneva) that India, Burma, and Indonesia (representing 700 million Asian people) refused to sign.

The United Nations, the world's "town meeting" forum, has been impotent, its spokesmen ignored. It has been impotent because of veto powers exercised in the Security Council and because three of the four warring groups (Saigon, Hanoi, and the NLF) are not member states. Time and time again, however, Secretary-General U Thant has sought to initiate peace moves (in retrospect, his recommendations have been altogether valid) only to be spurned by Washington. Outdated and disproven cold war dogmas were permitted to stand in the way of a political settlement.

We say we represent the free world in Southeast Asia. Yet, by our own definitions, the "free world" includes such countries as Brazil, Greece, Spain, and Turkey, an assortment of repressive military dictatorships. Our historic allies, Britain and France, have been bitterly critical of the arrogant unilateral interventionist policies of the super-powers.

I am not suggesting that communism represents freedom. The Soviet Union's rapacious conduct in Hungary and Czechoslovakia belies that romantic illusion. Forms of vigorous and inhumane repression go hand in hand with the kinds of control exercised by Peiping, Havana, Hanoi, and Warsaw. But, in Southeast Asia, where the people have no experience with democracy as we understand it, they have not been permitted to work out their own destinies, and, from their vantage point, the Saigon generals are puppets in the hands of

American interests. Once the generals fought by the side of the French against their own people. Now they are fighting under the direction of the Pentagon.

The very nature of the war in Vietnam is turning frightened, angry peasants into the arms of the communists. Michael Bernhardt, a veteran of My Lai who refused to take his rifle from his shoulder when unarmed women and children were being slaughtered, has said:

> It seemed everywhere we left, if the enemy wasn't there when we got there, he was there when we left. We seemed to be sort of growing them, planting them like seeds. Wherever we went we sort of bred the enemy. He just came out of nowhere, and it was almost as if we weren't there, there would be none.[7]

In a word, our policies and actions in Southeast Asia have divided the free world as nothing else since the end of World War II, have united tense and competing segments of the Communist world, and have *created* new "Communists" (at least fierce anti-American sentiments) among the peasant masses.

I have barely mentioned freedom in connection with Saigon. Apologists for the Thieu-Ky government are fond of appealing to the "free elections" of 1967. Let us look at three elections, including one that was never held. Freedom and self-determination were hardly served when Ngo Dinh Diem, guided and supported by the United States government, subverted the Geneva Accords by refusing to hold the 1956 elections. As President Eisenhower explained it, "Possibly eighty percent of the population would have voted for the Communist Ho Chi Minh as their chief of state." [8] Apparently we believed in self-determination only if we held the trump cards. Earlier, in 1955, Diem held his own elections in the South. He won an overwhelming victory. Out of 450,000 registered voters, he received 605,025 votes, which would have been impressive even in Cook County. Were those results a measure of freedom?

What about 1967? General "Big" Minh, the most popular foe of Marshal Ky in South Vietnam, was not permitted to run. Au Truong Thanh, a widely known neutralist (and anti-communist) who had served as Ky's finance minister, was not permitted to run. Truong Dinh Dzu, a run-of-the-mill lawyer who, midway through the campaign, began to talk about negotiations with the NLF, unexpectedly placed second. (He was promptly put in prison where he remains to this day.) Following a carefully managed campaign in which the political apparatus of village life, the communications media, and the United States presence were manipulated to serve the purposes of the Thieu-Ky ticket, that ticket was able to poll less than 35 percent of the popular vote. (And now the long-awaited presidential elections of 1971 have turned into a total fiasco.) In Paris we have repeatedly insisted that that government represents the people of South Vietnam, thus blocking the pathway to a negotiated settlement. And all in name of freedom.

Eighty percent of the people south of the 17th parallel are Buddhists. The vast majority of them are ardent nationalists, staunchly anti-Communist and bitterly anti-American. They have fought both Chinese invaders and French colonizers and have come to angrily resent our presence. They are a Third Force opposed to Communist terrorism *and* police-state repression. They have no government.

The Saigon generals are nonrepresentative—and repressive. There are thousands of non-Communist political prisoners in South Vietnam. There are thousands more non-Communists who are political exiles in France and elsewhere. The government closes down newspapers, outlaws student and veterans' organizations, silences "intellectuals" and old-guard nationalists, and refuses to permit any discussion of a coalition government. ("I'm too weak to cooperate in an accommodation with Communists," says President Thieu.[9]) Thieu uses military field courts, extra constitutional "kangaroo courts," to take care of his political opposition. And forms of abuse and physical torture are employed, as revealed when two United States congressmen stumbled onto the infamous "tiger cages" at the Con Son Island encampment for political prisoners. This is the "freedom" American taxpayers are purchasing and fifty thousand American soldiers have died to preserve.

Do we really believe in self-determination? We have repeatedly said so. If we do, it is difficult to dispute one of the conclusions of the Committee of Concerned Asian Scholars. Their study says: "Whatever the situation, the future of Vietnam should be determined only by the Vietnamese themselves. The American intervention stands as an enemy to Vienamese national self-determination, prohibits the expression of political forces in the South, and prolongs the agony of the war." [10]

Another myth: *We are in Southeast Asia for the sake of the people of Southeast Asia.*

A writer has said, "Only the most malicious of hypocrites can justify continued American involvement on grounds that the United States is 'defending the majority of the population' from this or that threat." [11] Harsh words, yet demonstrably true.

In Vietnam, American chemical attacks have ruined more than four million acres of arable land.[12] Mangrove forests and vital croplands have been destroyed. Millions of peasants have been driven from their ancestral homes and graveyards. They have been forcibly resettled in "refugee camps" [13] and "new life hamlets." The resettlement of peasants has been at the heart of a "pacification" program designed to separate the masses from the Viet Cong. However, as one South Vietnamese official put it, "Instead of separating the population from the Viet Cong we [are] making Viet Cong." [14] Thich Nhat Hanh, a Buddhist monk who now lives in exile in Paris, has written a poignant account of the plight of the Vietnamese peasant.[15] He reminds us that the peasant does not have the slightest idea what this war is all about. He does not know the difference between communism and capitalism. Do not talk to him about the sacred value of his property. He has been driven from it. Do not talk to him about Western-style democracy. He has never known it, and he does not want it. Right now, with growing fear and bitterness, he is only trying to stay alive.

The delicate fabric of traditional Vietnamese family relationships, village life, and Buddhist-Confucian values has been ripped to shreds. Cities are glutted with millions of anonymous refugees. Over the last decade Saigon has increased in size more than 500 percent and now has a population density of nearly 13,000 people per square mile. Shoeshine boys, pickpockets, barmaids, pimps, and prostitutes are among the highest paid workers in the land. A traditional civilization is being destroyed, only to be replaced by a social order catering to the needs of the ever-present American.

We are concerned, and rightly so, about 50,000 American soldiers killed and 1,600 prisoners of war being held in North Vietnam. We are concerned about the taxpayers' burden in the United States and the disarrangement of national priorities. But think of the Indo-Chinese! For twenty-five years they have been engaged in civil wars and have been fighting foreigners. According to some accounts more than a million people have been killed, *90 percent of them civilians.* The Kennedy subcommittee reported that there were 240,000 civilian casualties in South Vietnam in 1968 alone. South Vietnam is just one part of Indochina. *By 1970 (before the Laotian invasion) more bombs had been dropped in Laos than in both Vietnams.* The Plain of Jars had been virtually depopulated and countless villages had been "wasted." The "secret war" had already taken its toll.

In May of 1970, the same vicious, inhumane pattern was thrust upon Cambodia. Without bothering to consult allies, involved nations, or congressional leadership, bypassing the constitutional checks and balances designed by our forefathers, violating territorial boundaries and international law, the Nixon Administration sent our military machine into one more tiny, underdeveloped country half a world away. Once again search-and-destroy tactics ravaged the jungles as villages were burned, hamlets destroyed, and innocent civilians killed. The first body count we made after that invasion listed more than six hundred enemy dead. In that action, seven guns were found. How do you define an enemy? Who do you count? Richard Dudman, correspondent for the *St. Louis Post-Dispatch* who was seized and held for six weeks by Cambodian guerrillas, later wrote, "In this great migration [from areas of American aerial bombardment] we felt we were watching the terrorization of the peasants in Cambodia. We felt that we were observing the welding together of the local population with the guerrillas. The peasants were turning to the fighters once again." [16] In the words of Michael Bernhardt, "Wherever we went we sort of bred the enemy."

Are we in Indochina for the sake of the people there? The myth would be laughable if it were not so desperately tragic. Life-and-death decisions have long since been taken from their hands as the level of their suffering has intensified.

Finally, the overarching myth: *We are always "right," and "they" (however we choose to define the "enemy") are always wrong.*

Do you remember the "yellow peril" and the Huns; war bond posters showing Japanese soldiers with blood dripping from their fangs and Nazis who looked more like animals than men? Harry Truman, during the early days of the cold war, earnestly suggested that the United States represented the Sermon on the Mount while Russia symbolized the devil. Before any nation can justify the slaughter of an enemy, it must learn to fear and hate him. It cannot fear and hate him until he has been dehumanized. In Vietnam it is easier to "waste" a "gook" than to gun down a panic-stricken child, a sobbing mother, or a weary old man.

It was during the Second World War that sensitive Americans realized they, too, were capable of inhumanity. Germany had concentration camps; we had relocation centers. Saturation bombing leveled London; it incinerated Cologne, Dresden, Hamburg, and Tokyo. Auschwitz was heinous; so was Hiroshima. In 1937, when Hitler bombed Guernica with fire bombs, "a new passion of anger swept the world";[17] and now we use napalm in the jungles of Indochina. A friend returned from the South Pacific after World War II and described the gang-rape of a Japanese nurse his company had captured. He could not believe what he had seen; I could not believe what I heard. After all, the American GI is different. How can he be? War dehumanizes; it destroys people in countless ways.

Vietnam has brought all this into sharp, clear focus. The massacre at My Lai took place. An American captain allegedly ordered it. An American lieutenant with his "C" Company carried out the orders. More recently, the torture and murder of prisoners by South Vietnamese troops under the direction of American officers has been charged and documented by a rawboned, crew-cut, oft-decorated Vietnam veteran, Lt. Col. Anthony Herbert. Our vaunted body counts have included the kinds of people shot down at My Lai. But to blame atrocities on the senselessness of a war or the fear and battle-weariness of troops is not enough. "Free-fire zones," deliberate search-and-destroy battle tactics, the indiscriminate use of napalm and saturation bombing, and the increasing bitterness of an entire peasant population made My Lai and other similar tragedies inevitable.

Defenders of our policies and tactics talk about the violent inhumanity of communism. They point to instances of Vietcong terrorism. Crude bombs have been thrown into theaters, rockets have been dropped onto public parks, and village leaders have been murdered. There was the Hue massacre during the Tet offensive. Such recitals only emphasize my point. War creates warriors, it "justifies" terrorism and widescale killing, and it distorts and destroys moral considerations.

The technology of the Indo-Chinese war is a case in point. The B-52's and fleets of helicopters are *ours*. The napalm and CS gas are *ours*. The flamethrowers are *ours*. The folding-fin rockets and cluster bombs are *ours*. We have dropped twice the bomb tonnage on Vietnam that all the Allies dropped on all enemy targets during World War II. With the extension of the war into Cambodia and Laos, the air war is enlarged and intensified.

A specialist, describing the effects of our new and highly technical weaponry, writes:

[These new weapons] are primarily effective against decentralized agricultural populations; they devastate broad areas; . . . They are designed to be used against defenseless people; and they demand undisputed air superiority to be effective. Use of the weapons results in the indiscriminate slaughter of civilians and soldiers alike.[18]

Two years ago I walked through the stinking, sweltering corridors of a Saigon hospital. There I saw scores of little children, some whimpering, some staring through glazed eyes at nothing. Hands, arms, feet, and legs were missing. Blood and body liquids oozed through crude bandages. These were the trophies, the real victims, of a war like this.

On March 4, 1969, George Wald, professor of biology at Harvard and Nobel Prize winner, speaking to a group of scientists at MIT, said, "Our national symbols have gone sour. How many of you can sing about 'the rockets' red glare, the bombs bursting in air' without thinking, Those are *our* bombs and *our* rockets, bursting over South Vietnamese villages? When those words were written, we were a people struggling for freedom against oppression. Now we are supporting open or thinly disguised military dictatorships all over the world." [19]

To go back to the beginning: Southeast Asia has exposed the fatal error of many of our favorite myths. Are we mature enough, as a people, to acknowledge our tragic mistakes? The war in Vietnam has been wrong. Have we learned that the dangers inherent in the military/industrial complex, a continuation of outmoded and disproven cold war "logic," a disregard for principles of self-determination and the welfare of millions of helpless Asian people, and a recurring conviction that we are a superior breed and that our country is always more noble than its surrounding neighbors have brought us to our present crisis?

As Middle-American Christians—and as brothers of all men everywhere—we need to remind ourselves that:

History is under God's continuing judgment.

God serves the interests and pretensions of no single nation.

Southeast Asia is *our* problem, because human beings have been killed on both sides of the conflict and they are our brothers.

National repentance is called for.

Such repentance requires a re-examination and change of basic loyalties and values; our myths must be exploded.

A living, risen Lord stands in the midst of this catastrophe waiting to reconcile and rebuild through his servant people.

The Citizen's Conscience 12
☆☆☆☆☆☆☆☆☆☆☆

On March 16, 1968, Company C landed at a village called Song My in South Vietnam under orders to "destroy it and all its inhabitants." Private First Class Michael Bernhardt, a textbook soldier in almost every respect, trained by Green Berets in his Miami Reserve Officer Training Corps days, a student at LaSalle Military Academy before that, kept his rifle slung on his shoulder with its muzzle pointed to the ground. He refused to shoot old men and women and children. He refused to follow orders.

Paul David Meadlo, on the other hand, followed orders. His mother said, "I sent [the Army] a good boy and they sent home a murderer." The question: What is a soldier's responsibility—or for that matter, a citizen's responsibility—when his conscience comes into conflict with the laws of the state or the orders of governmental authority? The issue is not clear.

Socrates, standing before an Athenian tribunal, said, "I shall obey God rather than you. . . . Either acquit me or not; but

This paper was delivered at the Congressional Conference on War and National Responsibility, held in Washington, D.C., March, 1970. It appeared in the *Christian Advocate,* June 11, 1970 and, in a slightly different form, in the book *War Crimes and the American Conscience,* edited by Erwin Knoll and Judith Nies McFadden, published by Holt, Rinehart and Winston, Inc., copyright © 1970 by Congressional Forum. James Reston, Managing Editor of the *New York Times,* has called the book "the most important book on Vietnam in print today."

whichever you do, understand that I will never alter my ways, not even if I have to die many times." But, according to Plato, a month later in his death cell the same man said, "A man must do what his city and his country order him." [1]

Justice Abe Fortas, of much later vintage, does not help much. He wrote, "If I had lived in Germany [under Hitler] or had been a Negro living in Birmingham, . . . I hope I would have refused to wear an armband, to *Heil Hitler,* to submit to genocide. . . . I hope I would have disobeyed the state law that said I might not enter the waiting room reserved for 'whites.' " He goes on to say, however, that he would never condone "efforts to overthrow the government or to seize control of an area or parts of it by force" without explaining how there could be a mass protest against Nazi or racist oppression without the probability of "force" or violence.[2]

The conflict is an obvious one. Is the individual conscience of man ever justified in challenging and defying the collective conscience of the state? In a sense, the conflict pits legal structures, political realities, and social "stability" against the individual's sense of dignity, worth, "rightness," and personal responsibility.

Conceivably the state can epitomize bestiality, as it did in Nazi Germany. Its laws and customs can violate the free spirit of man, as in a military government, a communist police state, a racist nation or region, a segregated school district, or suburban housing development. Make no mistake about it. Historically, governments have betrayed "the common good" time and time again. *We can expect even the most enlightened state to protect its interests and preserve its structures by denying its citizens certain liberties.* To suggest that there is absolute individual freedom in the United States is transparently untrue. What of compulsory education, taxation, military conscription, and laws that dictate who a man will serve and sell to? What about a president who was not elected by a majority of the people; a costly, tragic war that has never been declared; our country's contribution to the international anarchy that makes each nation a law unto itself; and the possibilities of a push-button holocaust that could destroy us all quite apart from our individual knowledge of consent? At a more subtle level of public policy, what about the House Armed Services Committee, functioning behind closed doors, exercising unbelievable influence over defense budgets, national priorities, and the militarization of a nation —without *my* consent, without *your* consent?

There is no way for any man to be totally free. The individual's life is always conditioned by time, place, and circumstance. He can never extract himself from his cultural and political context. Granting the "givens" of his existence, what recourse has he to challenge the establishments of his world; to protest, to dissent, to declare his independence as his forefathers did? Well, he can throw the tea into Boston Harbor; he can defend Bunker Hill. If he does not feel impelled to go that far, he can follow the example of certain Quaker judges in colonial Pennsylvania (or more recently, Charles Lindbergh in his government's "defense" program) and simply withdraw from structured public responsibility rather than engage in procedures and policies his conscience rebels against. He can refuse to fire his gun, like Private First Class Bernhardt at My Lai; or resist the draft; or face court-martial proceedings because of his opposition to the Vietnam war, like Captain Howard Levy; or burn himself to death, like a Buddhist monk; or far this side of such a gesture, he can simply insist on doing his own thing in his own way.

The free man will not look to the state to "give" him his freedom. He will claim it, affirm it, make his decisions on the basis of it, and *willingly accept the consequences.* The man who functions on the basis of only those rights and liberties guaranteed by the state (whether he lives in Hanoi, Moscow,

Peiping, Saigon, or Kalamazoo) is not free. He has permitted the state to define the limits of his selfhood.

The free and responsible man will support and refine man-made laws wherever possible, but he will not permit his conscience to be limited by statute or its application. Milton Mayer says flatly, "Nuremberg was a sham." [3] That is not true. Surely the Nuremberg principles have exercised a restraining influence over the conduct of war and, on occasion, have encouraged dissent. But Nuremberg has been happily ignored by the CIA, "official" investigating teams and the administration-of-your-choice. Though we may appeal to sweeping investigations and trials, freedom does not find its ultimate security in legal procedures (as the trial of the Chicago Eight pointed out), or in formal precedent (as Nuremberg painfully reminds us).

If he is a religious man, the individual will appeal to transcendent authority and join St. Peter in saying, "We must obey God rather than man." He will "seek first" God's kingdom, insisting that every other loyalty is a lesser loyalty. Or, lacking the authority of revelation, he may join Thoreau in refusing to pay taxes, in denouncing legalized racism and an unjust war, in appealing to the "general right and obligation of men to disobey commands of a government" which they consider morally wrong.

Flag-waving chauvinism must be recognized for exactly what it is. If Auschwitz was inhumane, so was Hiroshima. If the murder of kulaks (middle-class Russians) was wrong in Stalin's Russia, so was the relocation of Nisei Americans during World War II. Viet Cong terrorism is harsh reality. The Hue massacre *happened* during the Tet offensive of 1968. But Viet Cong terrorism does not justify the Song My massacre, or the murder of Thai Khac Chuyen by the Green Berets (Chuyen's widow cried, "I thought they were saving us from the Viet Cong, but I see now that they are just as bad as the Viet

Cong."), nor does it justify General Thieu's "kangaroo courts." *Atrocities are not legitimatized by being Americanized.* William Lloyd Garrison said it far better than I: "Our country is the world, our countrymen are all mankind. . . . The interests, rights, liberties of American citizens are no more dear to us, than those of the whole human race."

Today *our* nation is involved in an immoral war in Southeast Asia. It is spending $70 billion a year on a war economy, permitting a military/industrial complex to dominate national policy with no effective system of checks and balances. While the Pentagon grows more truculent and the administration consciously escalates the arms race with its missile and anti-missile talk, the Vice-President of the United States (aided and abetted by Pat Buchanan) scatter-shots his charges, badgering the finest newspapers and the most responsible television commentators in the land, branding conscientious citizens "political hustlers," "merchants of hate" and "ideological eunuchs," and lashing out at what he calls the "whole damn zoo" of youthful dissenters.

It *can* happen here. It might well be *happening* here. Our nation is not the near Utopia envisioned by our forefathers. There is an essential place in this and every state for a Martin Luther King to write from his Birmingham jail: "I think we have moral obligations to obey just laws. On the other hand, I think we have moral obligations to disobey unjust laws because noncooperation with evil is just as much a moral obligation as cooperation with good." The lessons of the Third Reich may have slipped from our memories much too soon.

I am not an anarchist. I would, however, appeal to the Hegelian dialectic. If the thesis is the will of the state and the antithesis is the conscience of the individual, then I must come down firmly on the side of individual conscience. Only if individual liberties are stressed will the emerging synthesis reinforce the structures of freedom. The state has everything going for it—the military, the courts, unprecedented fiscal and political power, the entire sprawling apparatus of government. *In this kind of world, the individual must be encouraged to be true to himself;* this is the highest possible patriotism.

Henry David Thoreau was once scheduled to deliver an address called "A Plea for Captain John Brown." Sensing and reflecting the mood of the community, the sexton refused to ring the bell announcing the meeting, whereupon, Thoreau rang it himself. That is the acceptance of individual responsibility. There are bells to be rung, rights to be championed, causes to be served, and if we allow individual conscience to be swallowed up in the will of an impersonal state, then there will literally be hell to pay.

... Postscript on Lieutenant Calley 13
☆ ☆ ☆ ☆ ☆ ☆ ☆ ☆ ☆ ☆ ☆ ☆ ☆

This is a postscript. It is being added more than a month after the completed manuscript for *Mission: Middle America* had been mailed to the publisher. The reason for the addition is obvious. In the last chapter we discussed the citizen's conscience. Reference was made to My Lai and a GI's refusal to shoot innocent civilians. However, that paper was delivered at a congressional conference held long before the Calley court-martial. The trial of Lt. William L. Calley and the public uproar that followed the military court's verdict brought an assortment of issues into sharp and uncomfortable focus. There have been few times in this nation's recent history more appropriate for honest introspection; for literal *soul-searching*.

Certain facts stand out:

The Army, confronted with reports that Lieutenant Calley had shot and killed a large number of helpless villagers, was compelled to investigate those reports.

When incontrovertible evidence was produced, the Army charged Lieutenant Calley with a violation of military law and brought him to trial.

A panel of six officers (five were combat veterans who had served in Vietnam longer than Lieutenant Calley), after a four-month trial and thirteen days of agonizing deliberation, concluded that the lieutenant had indeed killed at least twenty-two civilians.

On the basis of the evidence, and in the light of martial

and international law, the military court at Ft. Benning sentenced the young officer to life imprisonment.

An overwhelming majority of the American people responded to the verdict with dismayed anger. According to a Gallup Poll, 79 percent of them disapproved of the court-martial decision and 83 percent supported President Nixon's intervention on the prisoner's behalf.

The facts are indisputable. Middle America's acceptance or rejection of the facts is a different matter and should require a season of honest self-appraisal on the part of thoughtful and conscientious citizens.

It is significant that perceptive journalists and returned servicemen have addressed the moral issues of Calley's role at My Lai with far more urgency and clarity than have religious leaders. (The voices of military chaplains have been disturbingly silent through all of this.) True, Billy Graham wrote about it, but his comments would offend no one, and the Very Rev. Francis B. Sayre, Jr., dean of the Washington Cathedral, offended nearly everyone when he wrote, "Calley is all of us." [1] Howard K. Smith, in a terse ABC-TV editorial rejoinder, said, "Calley is not *me*." But the journalists—Seymour Hersh, Jonathan Schell, Frank Harvey, Peter Arnett, Neil Sheehan, and others like them—have, on the basis of their reporting, brought the enormity of civilian suffering and the probability of widespread war crimes in Indochina to the doorstep of the American people. Keyes Beech, of the *Chicago Daily News*, began a penetrating column with the words "Before somebody proposes erecting a national monument to William L. Calley, Jr., the Vietnam War's leading anti-hero, there are a few things that ought to be said." [2] He went on to say them: (1) Lieutenant Calley got a fair trial, the longest in United States military history; (2) to portray Calley as an innocent victim of the system is a gross distortion of the facts; (3) the critics are correct when they say the Army taught

Calley to kill, but [it] did not send him to Vietnam to kill unarmed, unresisting women and children; (4) the insistence that the indiscrimate slaughter of "gooks" and "dinks" is not criminal is racism of the most vicious sort; (5) Calley was not a scapegoat singled out in order to free other war criminals; and (6) *the Calley verdict raises far-reaching questions of the morality or immorality of the Vietnam war, of who is guilty and who is not.*

It is this question of guilt that doubtless explains the uproar following the announced verdict. This question also has special relevance for the religious community. There are at least three levels of guilt involved in the My Lai massacre.

Individual guilt. To say that Lieutenant Calley was not guilty is to suggest that Nuremberg was a farce and that "the law of land warfare" included in the Department of the Army Field Manual is irrelevant and outdated. One hundred fifteen servicemen have been tried for the premeditated murder of Vietnamese civilians. Fifty-nine have been convicted of murder; twenty-one for lesser included offenses. In none of these cases did the number of deaths approach those allegedly resulting from Lieutenant Calley's action. Calley picked up a baby, threw him into a ditch and shot him. He butt-stroked an old man in the face and then shot away the side of his head at point-blank range. He "wasted" at least twenty-two lives and considered it "no big deal." The prosecutor of the Calley case, Capt. Aubrey M. Daniel, in his remarkable letter to President Nixon, wrote, "How shocking it is if so many people across this nation have failed to see the moral issue which was involved in the trial of Lieutenant Calley—that it is *unlawful* for an American soldier to summarily execute unarmed and unresisting men, women, children and babies." [3] To suggest that Lieutenant Calley should not be held responsible is to strip him of his personhood. Conditioned to react with callous violence? Undoubtedly.

Frightened and frustrated by the nature of the warfare? Undoubtedly. But, there were soldiers present who refused to fire. There were others, later, who could not live with the awful knowledge of their deed. We are moral creatures, responsible for our acts, or the Christian gospel is a lie and future prospects for the human family are bleak indeed.

If Lieutenant Calley's murderous conduct was shocking, the spontaneous reaction of the American people to the court-martial's verdict was equally so. It was as if the soldiers who refused to fire were the guilty ones; as if the jury of six men was guilty for acting on the basis of overwhelming evidence. Major Harvey G. Brown, one of the jurors, was asked by a television interviewer if the verdict was not a little harsh. Brown agreed, but reminded the interviewer that what Lieutenant Calley had done to the people in the ditch "was pretty harsh, too."

The guilt issue cannot stop with Lieutenant Calley. *Command guilt was also involved.* The Nazis condemned at Nuremberg were those responsible for the policies that resulted in atrocity. General Tomoyuki Yamashita was convicted and sentenced to death by a United States military commission following World War II (a decision upheld by the United States Supreme Court), because he failed to control the operation of his troops, "permitting them to commit" atrocities against civilians and prisoners of war. Apparently Yamashita had no knowledge of the atrocities committed in the Philippine Islands, but he was held accountable for them. If extended to My Lai, application of these precedents would implicate not only the field officers still awaiting trial, but also the chain of command leading to President Johnson himself.

My Lai should not be viewed in isolation. There have been many My Lais. The very nature of the war has made that tragic fact inevitable. More than a thousand Vietnam Veterans Against the War gathered in Washington in the spring of 1971 to dramatize their rejection of the war. One of their most conspicuous and eloquent leaders, an oft-decorated ex-Navy lieutenant, came to a point where he could not justify "shooting at targets we did not see, at the free-fire zones, at sampans." He said, "You might fire at an old grandmother or grandfather and you did not know if they were VC. *What was the morality of that?*" [4] Earlier, more than one hundred "winter soldiers" had testified in Detroit about their participation in war crimes in Vietnam, Cambodia, and Laos. There was talk of the "sport" of firing from helicopters at panic-stricken peasants scurrying for cover, and of the "need" to use civilians as human mine detectors in disputed war zones. Burke Marshall writes, "We know, or at least we should know, that the number of civilians that we are responsible for having killed, or disabled, or made parentless, or made childless, is far greater proportionately . . . than in any other war." [5]

In earlier chapters we have said it. Free-fire zones, search-and-destroy tactics, saturation bombing, highly technical anti-personnel weaponry, the assumption that the people (unless "pacified" in our centers or on our terms) are the enemy; our apparent willingness to see primitive lands and defenseless civilians destroyed in order to preserve our "national honor" —these are the ingredients that set the stage for war crimes. Thus, it is preposterous to place the sole blame for My Lai on the shoulders of Lieutenant Calley. What about those who have designed the nature of the war since its radical escalation: Robert S. McNamara, Dean Rusk, Walt W. Rostow, Townsend Hoopes, General Westmoreland, and our three most recent presidents? In the words of Neil Sheehan:

The cleansing of the nation's conscience and the future conduct of the most powerful country in the world towards the weaker peoples of the globe, demand a national inquiry into the war crimes question. *What is needed is not prison sentences and executions, but social judgments soberly arrived at, so that if these acts are war crimes future American leaders will not dare to repeat them.* (italics mine)

Lieutenant Calley's guilt has been determined. But who was responsible for Lieutenant Calley and for the nature of the war in which he found himself? This is a question that moves beyond Captain Medina, the late Lieutenant Colonel Barker, and General Koster, beyond the Pentagon and the White House to the American people themselves.

There is such a thing as *collective guilt.* This is especially true in a representative democracy. There was a time when the "silent majority," uninformed or misinformed, strongly supported this nation's unilateral intervention in Vietnam. Later, as harsh facts were revealed and cold logic applied, a mood of uneasy confusion swept across the land. Today, with most American people completely disenchanted with the war and with 70 percent of us agreeing that we cannot believe "official" versions of its conduct, we remain acquiescent and submissive. The silent majority maintains its silence, and the guilt becomes even more our own.

Perhaps guilt is too strong a word. We are not guilty as Lieutenant Calley was. We are not the architects of massive air cover and search-and-destroy strategies that are responsible for the slaughter of thousands upon thousands of simple peasants. But now we have been exposed to the realities of the war in Indochina; My Lai has seen to that. We find it almost impossible to accept a body of facts so grim and damning. That is one reason why the American people erupted when Calley was found guilty. Because, in a sense, we were found guilty, too. We are all involved in the war in Southeast Asia. Our sons and brothers have fought and died there. Our tax dollars have made the war possible. We have supported our leaders and defended their policies. Now, slowly and reluctantly, we are coming to see that we have been wrong, our policies have denied our national ideals, and the war itself has been the greatest crime of all.

What now are we to do as Middle Americans who profess to be Christian? *We must break our silence.* In the name of God we must speak out on behalf of our brothers everywhere, especially those who are the primary victims of a war they do not understand and cannot control. Middle America has tended to resent religious and political leaders who have "arrogated" to themselves the task of condemning present policies in the name of peace. Such persons have been considered troublemakers. Ironically, it is the peace-seekers who have been accused of polarizing the nation, while those who have defended and promoted the war have been lauded as our most solid citizens.

Gordon Zahn, a prominent Catholic layman, in an article appropriately called "The Church As Accomplice: Reflections on My Lai," referred to the "scandalous failures of the Catholic Church in Nazi Germany to give witness against the immorality of the Hitler regime and the injustice of its wars." [7] He went on to say:

The same scandal, the same failure is now ours. If we have now been forced to confess the parallel between My Lai and Lidice, we must also confess that it has its match in the refusal of our American bishops to protest the former, just as their German counterparts turned their eyes away from the latter. Actually, if we are honest, the American hierarchy suffers by comparison on two counts. First, at Lidice only males were "executed," whereas at My Lai the killing was indiscriminate so that even infants in their mothers' arms were not spared. Second, the German bishops knew that they and their flocks would face certain Gestapo retaliation had they chosen to protest; our American bishops cannot claim even that much "justification" for their silence. [8]

I am not a Roman Catholic, but I am an American bishop. I, and people like me in the heartland of this great nation, must seek God's forgiveness for our cautious silence. Probably most of the men involved in the My Lai massacre were church members back home. What had they learned in their Sunday school classes? What had they heard from their pulpits? What had their bishops said to them?

These are days for soul-searching in America. We are involved in an immoral war in which crimes are being committed against innocent people. A war criminal has been condemned, and vast numbers of us have cried out in angry protest. As a former Army officer put it, "My God, what has happened to us? How can Americans make a man a hero for killing helpless children?" They can't, and won't—not for long. But it is not enough to come to accept the guilt of Lieutenant Calley. We are all involved. If we are not guilty, we are at least *responsible*. The time has come for us to accept the full share of our responsibility and, in the name of God, to change direction.

Notes

Chapter 1

1. *Newsweek*, December 29, 1969, p. 19.
2. Colin Morris, *Include Me Out* (Nashville: Abingdon, paperback, 1968), pp. 11, 12-14.
3. George McGovern, Foreword, *The Urgent Now* by James Armstrong (Nashville: Abingdon, 1970), p. 9.
4. Morris, *Include Me Out*, p. 88.
5. SDS Port Huron Statement of 1962, p. 4.
6. Theodore Roszak, *The Making of a Counter Culture* (Anchor Book; Garden City, N. Y.: Doubleday, 1969), pp. 43-44.
7. Coretta Scott King, "The Legacy of Martin Luther King, Jr.," *Theology Today*, July 1970, p. 135.
8. *Ibid.*

Chapter 2

1. Quoted from Dr. Ford's address "The Church and Evangelism in a Day of Revolution," delivered at the U.S. Congress on Evangelism, Minneapolis, Minnesota, September 1969.
2. *Atlantic Monthly*, July 1970, p. 34.
3. *Newsweek*, February 1, 1971, p. 69.
4. Paul Tillich, *The New Being* (New York: Scribner's, 1955), p. 22.

Chapter 3

1. William C. Martin, "The God-Hucksters of Radio," *Atlantic Monthly*, June 1970, p. 51.
2. Quoted in "Social Reform: An Evangelical Imperative in the Crisis," *Good News*, October-December 1970, p. 74.

3. Emilio Willems, *Followers of the New Faith* (Nashville: Vanderbilt University Press, 1967), p. 134.
4. Quoted by Kevin and Dorothy Ranaghan, *Catholic Pentecostals* (Paperback; New York: Paulist/Newman, 1969), p. 141.
5. Marcus Bach, *The Inner Ecstasy* (Apex Book; Nashville: Abingdon, 1969), p. 197.
6. Brian Vachon, "The Jesus Movement Is upon Us," *Look,* February 9, 1971, p. 19.
7. From an address by John Mackay delivered at a symposium on The Churches and the Changing Social Order in Latin America, held in New York City, May 6-7, 1965.

Chapter 4

1. Claude Thompson, "Dilemmas of an Evangelical Christian," *Christian Advocate,* December 25, 1969, p. 8.
2. Arthur Gish, *The New Left and Christian Radicalism* (New York: Eerdmans, 1970), p. 94.
3. Quoted by José de Broucker, *Don Helder Câmara: The Violence of a Peacemaker* (New York: Orbis, 1971), p. 42.
4. Quoted by William Henzlik in articles appearing in the *Christian Advocate,* October 16, 1969, p. 24, and in *engage,* November 1, 1969, p. 16.

Chapter 5

1. *Newsweek,* October 6, 1969, p. 29.
2. *Ibid.,* p. 29.

Chapter 7

1. See Charles A. Reich, *The Greening of America* (New York: Random House, 1970).
2. Colin Morris, *Unyoung, Uncolored, Unpoor* (Nashville: Abingdon paperback, 1969), p. 96.
3. *Ibid.*
4. Nicolas Berdyaev, *The Realm of Spirit and the Realm of Caesar,* trans. Donald A. Lowrie (New York: Harper & Row, 1952), pp. 88-89.
5. *Chicago Daily News,* September 20, 1970, p. 8.
6. *New Left Notes,* June 20, 1969.
7. In *Issue One: Evangelism,* ed. Reuben P. Job and Harold K. Bales (Nashville: Tidings, 1970), p. 47.

Chapter 8

1. "As Clergymen Enter Politics—The New Trend," *U.S. News and World Report*, August 10, 1970, p. 19.
2. *New York Times Magazine*, October 4, 1970, p. 87.
3. "As Clergymen Enter Politics," p. 21.
4. Robert McAfee Brown, "An Open Letter to Spiro T. Agnew," *Christian Century*, October 14, 1970, pp. 12-13.

Chapter 9

1. Paul Ehrlich, *The Population Bomb* (New York: Ballantine, 1968), pp 18, 19.
2. Gordon Rattray Taylor, "The Threat to Life in the Sea," *Saturday Review*, August 1, 1970, p. 40.
3. Barry Weisberg, "The Raping of Alaska," *Ramparts*, January 1970, p. 33.
4. Gaylord Nelson, "Cleansing the Environment," *Playboy*, January 1971, p. 150.
5. Miller and Farnham, *The Ecology and Politics Manual*, p. 59.
6. Frederick Elder, *Crisis in Eden* (Nashville: Abingdon, 1970).
7. See Teilhard de Chardin, *The Phenomenon of Man* (New York: Harper Torchbook, 1961), p. 183; also Harvey Cox, *The Secular City* Rev. ed. (New York: Macmillan, [1964] 1966), p. 74.
8. Loren Eiseley, *The Firmament of Time* (New York: Atheneum, 1967) p. 8.
9. Rachel Carson, *The Silent Spring* (New York: Fawcett Crest Book 1964), p. 218.
10. Barry Commoner, *Science and Survival* (New York: Viking Press, 1963) p. 122.
11. "Affluence: The Fifth Horseman of the Apocalypse," *Psychology Today*, January 1970, p. 43.
12. *Ibid.*
13. Quoted in *The New Republic*, October 31, 1970, p. 14.

Chapter 10

1. Donald McDonald, "Militarism in America," *The Center Magazine*, January 1970, p. 12.
2. Knoll and McFadden, *American Militarism: 1970*, p. 11.
3. Richard J. Barnet, *The Economy of Death* (New York: Atheneum, 1969) p. 62.

4. Doug LeMaster, "Little Tree." This poem appeared in my earlier book *The Urgent Now* (Nashville: Abingdon, 1970), p. 49.

Chapter 11

1. Noam Chomsky, *American Power and the New Mandarins* (Vintage Book; New York: Random House, 1969), p. 4.
2. David Halberstam, "The Programming of Robert McNamara," *Harpers*, February 1971, p. 63.
3. *New York Times,* May 2, 1970.
4. See Richard J. Barnet and Marcus G. Raskin, *An American Manifesto* (New York: NAL Signet Book, 1970), p. 28.
5. Knoll and McFadden, *American Militarism: 1970,* p. 21.
6. Quoted in Victor Bator, *Vietnam: A Diplomatic Tragedy* (Dobbs Ferry, N. Y.: Oceana, 1965), p. 220.
7. *Evergreen,* April 1971, p. 57.
8. Dwight D. Eisenhower, *The White House Years,* Vol. 1, *Mandate for Change 1953-1956* (New York: Doubleday, 1963), p. 372.
9. Quoted in *Newsweek,* November 23, 1970, p. 63.
10. *The Indochina Story: A Fully Documented Account* (New York: Pantheon, 1971), p. 223.
11. *Ibid.,* p. xxiii.
12. See Ngo Vinh Long, *Thai-Bao-Ga,* November 5, 1969.
13. In Quang Ngai Province in 1967, there were sixty-eight refugee camps servicing 122,680 people. Fifty had no schools, forty-six had no latrines, and forty-two were without a medical dispensary. See Jonathan Schell, *The Military Half* (Vintage Book; New York: Random House, 1968).
14. Don Luce and John Sommer, *Vietnam: The Unheard Voices* (Ithaca, N.Y.: Cornell Paperback, 1970), p. 149.
15. Thich Nhat Hanh, *Vietnam: Lotus in a Sea of Fire* (New York: Hill & Wang, 1967), p. 64.
16. *New York Times,* June 24, 1970.
17. Philip Noel-Baker, quoted in *War Crimes and the American Conscience,* ed. Erwin Knoll and Judith McFadden (New York: Holt, Rinehart and Winston, 1970), p. 39.
18. *The Indochina Story,* p. 87.
19. Quoted in *The New Yorker,* March 22, 1969, p. 29.

Chapter 12

1. Quoted by Milton Mayer, *On Liberty: Man v. the State,* p. 17.
2. *Ibid.,* p. 9 n.

3. *Ibid.,* p. 96. I am indebted to Milton Mayer and the Center for the Study of Democratic Institutions for the "occasional paper" that proved so helpful in the preparation of this address.

Chapter 13

1. *New York Times,* April 5, 1971.
2. *Chicago Daily News,* April 6, 1971.
3. *New York Times,* April 7, 1971.
4. *Newsweek,* May 3, 1971, p. 25.
5. *New York Times,* April 10, 1971.
6. *New York Times Magazine,* March 28, 1971, p. 33.
7. *Worldview,* March 1971, p. 6.
8. *Ibid.*